Trauma and Self-Blame: Understanding the Psychological Impact on Men

Abstract

Survivors of adult sexual assault (ASA) and child sexual abuse (CSA) experience numerous negative consequences because of the violence they experienced. Self-blame is an important symptom to consider, and some research has shown certain characteristics may lead to increased trauma-related self-blame for survivors. High rates of self-blame are likely to lead to increased symptomatology and increased treatment resistance. The aim of this study was to explore the relationship between rape myth acceptance, tonic immobility, negative disclosure response experiences, substance use, and sexual arousal and how they may impact trauma-related self-blame for male survivors of adult sexual assault and/or child sexual abuse. 179 cisgender men with a history of CSA and/or ASA completed online measures to assess for rape myth beliefs, tonic immobility, disclosure experiences, sexual arousal, and substance use. Findings demonstrated that only rape myth acceptance significantly predicted self-blame in male survivors. Additionally, results indicated participants who used substances within 72 hours of their nonconsensual sexual event and previously disclosed their abuse experienced higher rates of self-blame than those who did not. Notably, even though sexual arousal was not a significant predictor in this study, only 2.8% of the total sample reported experiencing no indications of physiological sexual arousal and 60% had significant experiences of physiological sexual arousal. Additionally, over two thirds of the sample never disclosed the nonconsensual sexual event to anyone. Clinical implications and future research directions are discussed.

Table of Contents

List of Tables

List of Figures

Chapter I

Introduction

Nonconsensual sexual events or sexual victimization (SV) are terms used to describe any type of sexual activity in which consent is not freely given by one or more individuals (CDC, 2020). Sexual activity in this instance is a broad term which encompasses both contact and noncontact acts and spans across all gender identities and sexual orientations across the entire lifespan (NCIPC, 2019). Contact sexual acts are what are more commonly understood as sexual assault or rape, which can include kissing, fondling, penetrative intercourse, forced oral sex, or any other acts which involve direct physical contact (Peterson et al., 2011). Noncontact sexual victimization can include forcing someone to watch explicit sexual material, sexual harassment, and any other acts not involving direct physical contact (RAINN, 2019). SV often involves different forms of coercion, power, control, and manipulation by the perpetrator to satisfy their own desires and sexual gratification without concern or regard for the victim (Bullock & Beckson, 2011).

Numerous governmental agencies and researchers have made estimates about the total number of individuals who have experienced nonconsensual sexual events, but these statistics are likely underestimations of the true number of people who have experienced SV in the U.S., due to challenges surrounding disclosure (Smith et al., 2018). Much of the research literature has focused on female survivors of SV, and there is a need for more studies of male survivors. The prevalence rates of SV are shocking, with some estimates revealing 1 in 6 men will experience child sexual abuse (CSA) and 1 in 14 men have been forced to penetrate someone else during their lifetime (CDC, 2020).

The negative impact for individuals who experience SV of any form are immense. Mental health challenges, difficulties with relationship development, and general functioning challenges can span across the entire lifetime (Payne et al., 2014). Both men and women may experience significant sexual dysfunction after SV (Payne et al., 2014; Suschinsky & Lalumiere, 2011). Over 94% of female survivors of sexual assault meet diagnostic criteria for posttraumatic stress disorder (PTSD), 70% of all survivors experience severe emotional distress, and survivors are at significantly increased risk of using substances and are 10 times more likely to use major drugs than the general population, with a 19% substance use disorder rate among survivors (Dworkin, 2020; RAINN, 2019). Additionally, survivors of SV may experience physical health problems including cardiovascular disorders, gastrointestinal issues, and reproductive challenges (CDC, 2020).

Not only do nonconsensual sexual events have a detrimental impact on the survivor, but these experiences may also negatively impact close family members and friends of the survivor who may feel a burden of responsibility and the weight of shame and guilt (NSVRC, 2019). Sexual violence is also considered a nationwide public health crisis, costing public agencies millions of dollars each year (RAINN, 2019). Even though changes have been made in legal policies, the general population's understanding has grown, and various cultural reforms have occurred, sexual victimization continues to impact individuals of every cultural background at tremendously high rates (Loder & Robinson, 2020; Pratt, 2022).

Survivors of nonconsensual sexual events are more likely to endorse high levels of self-blame than survivors of any other forms of abuse, assault, or violence (Sigurvinsdottir & Ullman, 2019). Self-blame decreases the likelihood that survivors will disclose their assault and get the therapeutic support they need, leading to further distress, prolonged psychological symptoms, treatment resistant symptomatology, and increased risk for revictimization (Bhuptani & Messman, 2021). Because of self-blame and other similarly related factors, survivors may be unwilling and unable to even recognize the SV they experienced as assault, leading to unacknowledged rape and further social withdrawal, isolation, and substance use (Wilson et al., 2017). For men, rape acknowledgement, disclosure rates, and treatment seeking behaviors are even lower (Reed et al, 2020).

Many men are forgotten survivors. There is significant bias that exists when it comes to men who have experienced nonconsensual sexual events (Walker et al., 2019). Research has shown that various agencies, including hospitals, law enforcement, and even community rape crisis centers, do not provide services to male survivors and are often less likely to believe reports of sexual assault perpetrated against men (Bullock & Beckson, 2011). Although awareness of the sexual abuse of boys and men has been growing in recent years, there remains more significant stigma surrounding male survivors' experiences, leading to delayed disclosure rates, especially for CSA survivors (Easton et al., 2014). Some men have shared how their experiences of disclosing their SV were so negative they experienced secondary victimization from friends, family members, and even treatment providers, leading to even further increased feelings of violation and disappointment, self-blame, depression, and anxiety (Jackson et al., 2017).

Factors which directly contribute to higher rates of self-blame and shame are still not well understood within the research literature. More recently, research has shown that female survivors who had negative disclosure experience(s), who were under the influence of substances before/during the assault, and who experienced TI (TI) during the assault are likely to have higher levels of self-blame that female survivors who did not have these specific factors (Pratt,

2022). TI is phenomenon that involves partial or full body paralysis that leaves an individual completely unable to control their body when faced with a situation that elicits extreme fear (Abrams et al., 2009). There have been some indications that additional factors may also contribute to the development of self-blame for survivors. Rape myth acceptance (RMA) and unacknowledged rape are two factors which are likely to increase a survivor's self-blame (Romero-Sanchez et a., 2018). Additionally, individuals who experience sexual arousal and/or orgasm during their nonconsensual sexual event(s) are more likely to question the nature of the assault, avoid disclosing their abuse, and blame themselves for the experience (Bunderson, 2019). Most of the previous research has explored self-blame in female survivors, with much less research examining the factors leading to self-blame in male survivors; hence, there is a significant need for this research. It is important for clinicians, specifically mental health providers, to understand the complexity of sexual trauma and how these experiences may impact each survivor's unique presentation and clinical needs. Many treatment providers may not understand the importance and necessity of addressing sensitive topics such as sexual arousal, substance intoxication, rape myth acceptance, and TI with their male clients who have experienced SV, and until these topics are explored, many clients may not receive the full benefit from their therapeutic interventions.

Statement of Problem

Over 3%, or 1 in 33, men throughout the United States have experienced an attempted or completed rape after the age of 18 (RAINN, 2017). Additionally, male victims of CSA range from 2% to 31% of the total population (Matthews & Collin-Vezina, 2019). Over 21% of transgender, genderqueer, and gender nonconforming individuals have been sexually assaulted (RAINN, 2017). Sexual victimization is a widespread issue, impacting a large portion of the population. Each of these nonconsensual sexual events is unique, dependent on various situational, perpetrator, and victim characteristics, but there may be trends and patterns across these events that are important to explore (Bhuptani & Messman, 2021). Specifically, research is starting to identify specific factors which may increase the rate of self-blame experienced by survivors.

Factors which lead to increased self-blame are important to explore, as self-blame may cause survivors to be more reserved in the information they share with clinicians, leading to a lack of awareness of the full picture for treating providers, and increasing risks for revictimization (Miller et al., 2007). There is research showing that certain factors may be predictive of higher rates of self-blame. One factor, rape myth acceptance (RMA), or belief in false narratives regarding rape victims being at fault for their assault, may impact how survivors perceive and even acknowledge their rape, leading them to believe they hold responsibility and fault for the event (Wilson et al., 2017). Among individuals who are survivors of SV, many may feel paralyzed (i.e., TI) during the event, which has been shown to increase vulnerability to self-blame as well (Galliano et al., 1993). Research has also shown that approximately half of the individuals who have experienced sexual assault consumed alcohol and/or elicit substances directly before the assault, but findings are varied on the impact substances may have on post-assault functioning (Lorenz & Ullman, 2016). Additionally, survivors who endorsed physiological sexual arousal during their assault, are also much less likely to disclose and tend to display higher rates of self-blame (Bullock & Beckson, 2011). Lastly, of the individuals who did disclose their nonconsensual sexual event(s), negative responses to these disclosures impacted mental health symptoms, including the level of self-blame the survivors endorsed (Littleton, 2010).

Psychologists and other mental health providers must obtain a better understanding of how factors such as RMA, TI, disclosure experiences, substance use, and sexual arousal impact levels of self-blame. It is especially important to better understand how the manifestation of self-blame may differ between male and female survivors of CSA and ASA. Although there are many beneficial trauma-focused treatments being readily utilized in the field of psychology, these treatments often do not place a heavy emphasis on addressing feelings of self-blame (Pratt, 2022). The need for current research exploring factors contributing to self-blame among male survivors of ASA and CSA is of particular importance given the high prevalence and dearth of research. Male nonconsensual sex research is much less prevalent than female research and these specific variables have not been explored together to determine the impact they may have on male survivor's self-blame.

Literature Review

Childhood Sexual Abuse (CSA)

Over 17.7 million females and 2.8 million males in the U.S. have reported experiencing their first completed or attempted rape before the age of 18 (NSVRC, 2019). According to the U.S. Department of Health and Human Services, Administration for Children, Youth, and Families (2021), children aged three-years-old and younger were the most likely to experience some form of child maltreatment, which includes neglect, physical abuse, sexual abuse, and psychological abuse (CWIG, 2021). The trends in reported cases of maltreatment of children have been decreasing from 1990 to 2019, with sexual abuse rates having a reported 62% decrease (CWIG, 2021). Although these statistics may seem hopeful for the future, many researchers and clinicians within the field argue these reports may not be presenting the full picture of the severity and widespread nature of CSA and other forms of abuse, as only substantiated or indicated child maltreatment cases are reported in the national statistics and any unproven or unfounded cases are not (Canton-Cortez & Canton, 2010). Additionally, these statistics may be even less representative for male survivors, who are much less likely to disclose (Easton, 2012). In 2019, the National Child Abuse and Neglect Data System (NCANDS) found that 9.3% of the total population of children experienced some form of CSA before the age of 18, with 82% of the victims identifying as female (U.S. Department...2022; RAINN, 2017). Even if these statistics are not fully accurate, there are still a reported 57,329 children sexually abused each year and the issue of CSA is widespread enough to cause financial burden which reaches the level of a national crisis (RAINN, 2017). In 2015 alone, there were 40,387 substantiated cases of non-fatal CSA and 20 fatal cases of CSA across the U.S., leading to a significant financial burden of over $9.3 million from healthcare, special education, child welfare, suicide, and violence/crime costs, as well as productivity losses (Letourneau et al., 2018).

Similar to ASA, CSA has varying definitions within the literature. A common definition of CSA is any sexual act perpetrated against a child which includes but is not limited to fondling; intercourse; forced witnessing of masturbation or forced masturbation; obscene conversations via phone, text, or other digital mediums; producing, owning, or sharing pornographic images or clips of children; sex of any kind; sex trafficking; and any other forms of sexual contact (RAINN, 2017). Stated in broader terms, "CSA is any sexual activity perpetrated against a minor by threat, force, intimidation, or manipulation" (Collin-Vezina et al., 2013, p. 1).

Although definitions of CSA have lacked consistency, a shift to a more inclusive understanding of CSA has been made in recent years to include additional non-contact sexual activities which are considered abusive and reside within the category of CSA (Collin-Vezina et al., 2013). Previous definitions of CSA did not include any activities besides contact sexual activities, thus eliminating many abused children who did not fit the criteria (Collin-Vezina et al., 2013).

The importance of accurately and consistently defining CSA lies in the ability for this universal definition to help develop and improve policy, which may aid in early identification, prevention, and responses to CSA (Matthews & Collin-Vezina, 2019). Additionally, creating a universal definition that is all encompassing of the wide variety of sexually abusive acts survivors may have experienced can lead to increased understanding of the uniqueness and differences amongst these diverse experiences, which may lead to better tailored treatment approaches created for the survivors' individual experiences (Canton-Cortez & Canton, 2010). By creating a broader and more fully inclusive understanding of CSA, clinicians may become better equipped to treat survivors with diverse experiences. CSA is not only a national crisis leading to a significant financial burden placed on both systems and individuals, but it is hugely detrimental experience(s) that may impact survivors well into their adult lives.

Consequences of CSA. CSA is likely to lead to numerous mental, physical, and emotional challenges starting in childhood and continuing into adulthood if appropriate interventions are not received (Katz et al., 2020). Survivors of CSA are consistently shown to have higher rates of trauma-related symptoms, decreased self-esteem, denial, self-blame, self-isolation, emotional suppression, increased engagement in dangerous and risky behaviors, and diagnoses of PTSD, depression, anxiety, and substance use disorders (SUD; Canton-Cortez & Canton, 2010; Sanjeevi et al., 2018). Meta-analyses of CSA have reported short-term and long-term consequences beyond mental health diagnoses, including interpersonal difficulties and overall challenges with social functioning, developmental of chronic illnesses, and school/work related dysfunction, including loss of jobs and early school dropout (Hailes et al., 2019). Adults who experienced CSA are significantly more likely to experience various social functioning issues, including parenting challenges, lack of relationship satisfaction, difficulty with relationship adjustment, and challenges developing intimacy in romantic relationships (Sanjeevie et al., 2018). According to one study conducted with a cohort of sexually abused children across 43 years, when compared to a cohort of non-sexually abused children, the survivors had much higher rates of contact with community mental health services, representing 23.3% of the CSA survivors and 7.7% of non-abused individuals (Cutajar et al., 2010). Early experiences of CSA are also likely to increase survivors' rates of revictimization across their lifespan if they do not seek out appropriate support early on (Sanjeevi et al., 2018).

The evidence for the detrimental effect of CSA has been widely researched in various forms across diverse groups of survivors, but most of the research has been conducted on White, cisgender female survivors. Less is understood about why some survivors develop more severe symptoms and other survivors develop few or no symptoms, but various factors have been explored (Ventus et al., 2017). Numerous factors may impact the severity of symptom development, including perpetrator characteristics (e.g., closeness of relationship, coercion and fear inducing tactics used) and situational factors including severity and frequency of the abuse and the amount of force used during the abuse (Ullman et al., 2014). Research has shown that type and severity of the abuse may have an impact on symptom development, with more severe forms of abuse (i.e., anal, vaginal, or oral penetration) resulting in worse symptoms and more psychological distress in childhood than other less severe forms of abuse (i.e., non-contact abuse, folding, groping; Sanjeevi et al., 2018). Additionally, for both male and female survivors, earlier age of onset, high frequency and duration, use of physical force, perpetration by a relative or close friend, and penetration/contact abuse are most likely to lead to the worst outcomes for survivors, which may include more severe mental and physical health symptoms (Pratt, 2022; Zink et al., 2009). Some research suggests that CSA not only alters children's emotional states but also their cognitive states, leading to distorted self-concept and affective capacities that do not line up with the reality of the world (Collin-Vezina et al., 2013).

Research has shown the consequences of CSA may differ across gender, race, ethnicity, and numerous other cultural factors. Gray and Rarick (2018) examined the differences in the detrimental effects, specifically maladaptive coping, of CSA survivors in a sample of 13,583 male and female high school students. The findings indicated male survivors more frequently utilized substances to cope, whereas female survivors more frequently coped by engaging in self-harm behaviors or utilizing depressive withdrawal behaviors. The results did not indicate any specific coping differences between the White and Latinx participants (Gray & Rarick, 2018). Additional research has shown that cultural and familial values may play a role in how CSA is perceived, disclosure rates, and perceptions of the abuse, with some cultures holding values around modesty, virginity, and shame surrounding sexual activity or the discussion of sexual abuse (Fontes & Plummer, 2011; Yuksel, 2000).

Male survivors may also experience unique struggles after abuse related to societal expectations of conventional masculinity, which may lead to feeling the need to reframe their experiences of helplessness and vulnerability using denial and emotional suppression (Payne et al., 2014). Payne and colleagues' (2014) qualitative study of male CSA survivors found racial and ethnic differences in the survivors' experiences across themes of emotional and psychological distress, drug and alcohol use or abuse, communication issues, and more. Latino men had the easiest time with emotional identification and expression of their psychological issues, specifically talking about anger/rage, and guilt, shame, and regret and endorsing hypervigilance and flashbacks. Whereas White men struggled most with negative schemes about the self, including low self-esteem, increased self-hatred, and beliefs that they received the abuse due to being inherently bad (Payne et al., 2014). Black men, in general, were the least likely to identify current psychological distress, which the authors proposed may have been an effect brought about by lifetime histories of racial micro-aggressions, disrespect of personal dignities, and patterns of disregard by doctors and mental health professionals (Payne et al., 2014).

In both ASA and CSA, there appears to be a bi-directional relationship between number of nonconsensual sexual events experienced and levels of self-blame. This means that as individuals experience revictimization they are likely to have higher levels of self-blame and high levels of self-blame place survivors at higher risk of being revictimized (Miller et al., 2007). Sexual revictimization is common among survivors of both ASA and CSA. One study found that in survivors of CSA, an average of 47.9% of participants reported at least one revictimization experience, with rates ranging from 10.0% to 90.3% across over 80 studies of SV in childhood (Walker et al., 2019). It is important to more directly evaluate the relationship between number of nonconsensual sexual events and the impact this may have on survivors' level of self-blame, as well as how higher rates of self-blame may increase future risk for survivors.

Adult Sexual Assault (ASA)

Every sixty-eight seconds someone in the U.S., ranging in ages from young children to older adults, is sexually assaulted (RAINN, 2017). Oftentimes, language such as rape or sexual assault are used interchangeably throughout literature and social circles. It is important to note, that although rape is a form of sexual assault, there are many other forms of sexual assault as well (Peterson et al., 2011). Definitions of sexual assault vary across the research literature, with some authors arguing that for something to be considered sexual assault, an aspect of violent physical force must be included (Cunradi et al., 2005). Other people argue sexual assault can encompass any unwanted sexual acts, including verbal persuasion, witnessing masturbation, viewing unwanted sexual materials, groping, fondling, and other actions (Smith et al., 2018).

A universal definition of sexual assault does not exist, with many researchers relying on legal definitions of rape when discussing the broader acts of sexual assault, leading to possible confusion and misunderstanding (Peterson et al., 2011). One issue with using legal definitions of rape for research studies is that the definition varies from state from state in the United States. Another issue with using legal rape definitions when studying sexual assault is that many of these definitions require the victim to be penetrated by a penis, leading to exclusion of many survivors of sexual assault (McLean, 2013). Using this definition immediately excludes male survivors who were victimized by women or individuals who experienced other forms of sexually violent and assaultive acts (Forsman, 2017). Utilizing inclusive language and definitions when engaging in sexual assault research is important to assure accurate information and results are being presented. For the purposes of this study, a combination of the definitions of ASA provided by Forsman (2017) and Smith and colleagues (2018) will be used. These authors describe ASA as encompassing all forms of SV, which includes the legal definition of rape committed against men, "penile, digital, or foreign object penetration of the victim's mouth or anus through the use of force, coercion, violence, threats of violence, or incapacitation" (Forsman, 2017, p. 442). Additionally, this definition includes fondling, groping, oral-genital contact or any other forms of unwanted sexual acts or non-contact sexual events that do not necessarily have to have been obtained through the use of force (Forsman, 2017; Smith et al., 2018). Lastly, this definition includes nonconsensual kissing and witnessing of masturbation, flashing, and/or forcing individuals to look at or participate in generating sexually explicit material (Smith et al., 2018).

ASA is a public health crisis, with 17-25% of women and 1-3% of men experiencing sexual assault across their lifespan (Dworkin et al., 2017). It should be noted, these rates may not be a fully accurate depiction of the true number of sexual assaults, due to many survivors (especially men) never disclosing their assault (Easton et al., 2014). According to the National Sexual Violence Resource Center (NSVRC, 2019) rates of sexual assault can be as high as 24.8% of men in the U.S. Out of all the men and women who experience sexual assault or rape over 50% of these survivors were assaulted by either a friend or acquaintance (NSVRC, 2019). Rates of sexual assault are highest among individuals aged 18-24 (RAINN, 2017). For women, lifetime prevalence of sexual assault is 22.0% for Black individuals, 18.8% for White individuals, and 14.6% for Hispanic individuals (Black et al., 2011). Native Americans are at the highest risk for ASA and are two times more likely to experience ASA than any other racial group, with 56.1% of women and 27.5% of men experiencing some form of SV (NSVRC, 2019; RAINN, 2017). LGBTQIA+ individuals are also at a higher risk of SV. In a sample of Black and multiracial individuals, 27% of transgender and gender queer participants and 14% of cisgender participants reported being forced to engage in unwanted sexual activities (NSVRC, 2019). Although these statistics are helpful in understand the scope of the problem, a detailed breakdown of male survivors of ASA is much harder to come across.

Consequences of ASA. The consequences of ASA are vast and wide reaching and may be both short and long-term. These may include symptoms such as increased fear, anxiety, depression, suicidality, substance use, and posttraumatic stress, as well as decreased social functioning, self-esteem, and sexual dysfunction (Elliot et al., 2004). Many individuals who survive sexual assault are at an increased risk of developing not only psychological disorders but medical, sexual, and behavioral disorders as well (Cook et al., 2018). According to two research studies, across numerous forms of psychopathology, sexual assault survivors were significantly more symptomatic than their unassaulted comparison group, with 73-82% developing clinically significant anxiety disorders (Campbell et al., 2009; Dworkin et al., 2017). Survivors of sexual assault also tend to experience higher rates of PTSD and eating disorders when compared to individuals who have experienced other forms of assault or abuse (Campbell et al., 2009; Dworkin, 2020).

Although a complete understanding of why some survivors develop severe symptomatology and others do not has yet to be established, there are certain factors that may lead to worse symptoms for survivors of ASA. Differing traumatic experiences may be the result of certain assault characteristics, such as the severity or the assault, force used during the assault, and other factors, as well as characteristics of the individual survivors, including any prior sexual abuse and various demographic factors (Pratt, 2022). Additionally, certain demographic groups may have unique stigma surrounding sexual assault, which is not present in other cultural groups or with other forms of assault, likely leading to increased self-blame and shame for survivors (Bhuptani & Messman-Moore, 2019). An important demographic factor to consider in the discussion of consequences of ASA is biological sex or binary gender. Much of the previous research on consequences of ASA has been focused on female survivors who were victimized by men, with much less focus placed on male survivors (Peterson et al., 2011). Men may be more likely to endorse socially acceptable mental health challenges, such as anger issues or substance abuse, whereas they may be much less likely to endorse other symptoms such as anxiety, sadness, hopelessness, guilt, and shame (Helgeson, 2002). Some research has revealed that male survivors of ASA may actually have worse symptoms and outcomes than female survivors specifically related to sexual functioning, partly due to decreased treatment seeking behaviors and lower rates of disclosure (Elliot et al., 2004). Hlavka (2016) found that men who survived sexual assault were unable to rectify the incompatibility of traditional masculinity and sexual victimization, leading to increased self-blame, guilt, and shame. Additionally, research has shown that more traditional male attitudes have not been related to resilience, but gender self-acceptance may play a strong role in recovery and resilience related to both ASA and CSA (Graves et al., 2017). Resiliency factors, while important, are beyond the scope of the present study.

Trauma-Related Self-Blame

The idea of trauma-related self-blame is similar to self-blame in other situations; the individual holds beliefs that they themselves are somehow responsible for whatever happened (Lutz-Zois et al., 2015). In some cases, this blame may be accurately and appropriately directed to the self, but in most cases, these beliefs are inaccurate cognitive appraisals of the situation, leading to inappropriate self-blame, guilt, and shame, which is the case in sexual abuse and all other forms of abuse (Ullman et al., 2014). This self-blame may also be strongly related to societal and cultural views, specifically rape myths, in which the survivor is frequently blamed for the sexual assault or abuse because of reckless behaviors, being under the influence of substances, or other similar factors (Peter-Hagene & Ullman, 2018).

Rates of self-blame tend to be highest in survivors of nonconsensual sexual events due to survivors' inaccurate appraisals as well as societal support of rape myths, leading survivors to believe they should and could have done more to stop the abuse or that they were actually willing participants, even though coercion and manipulation were involved (Pratt, 2022; Spencer et al., 2017). Trauma-related self-blame also appears to vary across facets of diversity, with some research supporting higher rates of self-blame in Black women when compared to White women and higher rates in male survivors when compared to female survivors (Sigurvinsdottir et al., 2020; Sorsoli et al., 2008). Additionally, factors which may lead to increased self-blame for survivors of sexual assault include negative reactions from others, the survivor being under the influence of substances at the time of the assault, TI experiences during the assault, RMA, victim sexual arousal, and lack of previous disclosure (Bunderson, 2019; Peter-Hagene & Ullman, 2018; Pratt, 2022; Reed et al., 2020). Specific cultural factors may also play a role in the development of self-blame; specifically, cultures which hold stronger shame-based ideals, or adhere strongly to patriarchal hierarchical structures (Pratt, 2022). For children who survived CSA, predictors of higher self-blame include abuse severity and avoidance-based coping strategies surrounding abuse experiences (Quas et al., 2003).

It is important to differentiate between the two specific subtypes of self-blame, characterological self-blame (CSB) and behavioral self-blame (BSB; Janoff-Bulman, 1979). CSB is specific beliefs and attributions about oneself, or the character traits of the self, specifically the individual may believe they possessed certain traits that made them more likely to get abused or would predispose them to victimization (Peter-Hagene & Ullman, 2018). This type of self-blame often leads survivors to believe they were deserving of the assault and the assault was a result of who they are as a person, rather than situational factors or the abuser. They may view themselves as having inherently bad character and believe statements such as "I'm a bad person, thus I deserved to be assaulted" (Peter-Hagene & Ullman, 2018; Sigurvinsdottir & Ullman, 2014). At the core of this type of self-blame is the belief that who they are is the reason the abuse occurred (Sigurvinsdottir & Ullman, 2014). With BSB, the focus of the self-blame is on the situational factors of the event or choices the individual made before and during the assault, rather than more personal, character-based factors (Sigurvinsdottir & Ullman, 2014). If survivors are experiencing BSB, they may believe statements such as "I shouldn't have been at that place or trusted that person," they may blame themselves for drinking too much, being too reckless, or numerous other behaviors (Peter-Hagene & Ullman, 2018).

Trauma-related self-blame is an important topic of discussion and consideration because it frequently leads to poor psychological adjustment, specifically worse PTSD symptomatology, maladaptive coping strategies, and reduced disclosure rates (Ullman et al., 2014). Research has shown that internalized self-blame is likely to increase the risk of revictimization, with revictimization then further reinforcing the self-blame, which leaves survivors locked into this negative cycle (Bernstein et al., 2022; Breitenbecher, 2006). Although the research has varied as to the outcomes when survivors experience high levels of self-blame, with some research supporting only CSB leading to worse outcomes, whereas other studies found that both CSB and BSB increase future risk and lead to more severe symptoms, there is research to support the overall negative impact of self-blame (Sigurvinsdottir & Ullman, 2014; Ullman et al., 2014). Most of the research has shown that CSB leads to poorer outcomes, whereas BSB could potentially act as a protective factor for survivors. The argument for these research findings is that it is much easier to change one's behavior (i.e., BSB) than it is to change who one is (i.e., CSB; Sigurvinsdottir et al., 2020).

One study, conducted by Sigurvinsdottir and colleagues (2019), found that for Black women, CSB was predictive of increased psychological symptoms, including PTSD and depressive symptoms, whereas BSB was not. Their findings indicated that only CSB led to increased suicidal ideation for the participants. The authors argued that this participant group of

Black women likely experienced higher suicidal ideation due to the interaction between CSB and the racial marginalization and discriminatory experiences they faced throughout their lives (Sigurvinsdottir et al., 2019). Another study of 416 college-aged women found a significant correlation between the Global Severity Index of the Symptom Checklist-90-Revised (SCL-90-R), which is a broad measure of psychological distress, and CSB, $r = .29$, $p < .05$ (Breitenbecher, 2006). Finally, CSB has also been seen to be highly predictive of PTSD symptomatology whereas BSB has not, which does not appear to vary across race, age, or educational status (Peter-Hagene & Ullman, 2018).

Rape Myth Acceptance

On specific area of stigma that may lead to increased shame and guilt for survivors is the concept of rape myths or RMA (Walfield, 2018). Rape myths are false, widely accepted beliefs which contribute to normalizing sexually violent behaviors by offenders and focus on the negative actions and behaviors of survivors (Lonsway & Fitzgerald, 1994). Some common rape myths include: she (note that many measures assume a female survivor) asked for it due to the clothes she was wearing, being intoxicated/high, or other behaviors she displayed, men cannot be raped, if someone doesn't fight their attacker off, it wasn't rape, and once a man is sexually aroused, he can't himself and he has to have sex (Suarez & Gadalla, 2010). Again, many measures of rape myths use gendered language and are focused on females as victims and males as perpetrators (Johnson et al., 2021) More specifically, these rape myths reinforce placing blame and fault on survivors of ASA and relieving the offenders and serve as "justification for one's decision to rape" (Lutz-Zois et al., 2015, p. 85). Research has shown that female survivors of ASA are likely to feel that others would blame them for the assault if they were to disclose, they would not be believed, and there would be other negative consequences to their social and work lives, which led many of these survivors to place blame on themselves for their sexual assault (Burns et al., 2014). RMA also tends to be much higher when survivors were under the influence of substances during the time of the sexual assault and observers are much less likely to intervene and more likely to blame the survivor (Romero-Sanchez et al., 2018).

High rates of RMA may also be tied to religious communities, specifically the Christian population, who strongly support purity culture, leading to an increased likelihood of labeling sexual assault and rape as consensual sexual experiences (Owens et al., 2020). A commonly held rape myth regarding female survivors of sexual assault is that the woman provoked her sexual assault by the way she dressed, acted, or portrayed herself to the offender (Lutz-Zois et al., 2015). Sexual assault is the only form of violence in which the victim is questioned on personal factors related to clothing choices or other similar factors (Pratt, 2022).

RMA has been shown to lead to much higher rates of unacknowledged rapes, which is when a nonconsensual sexual event has occurred, but the survivor does not acknowledge the victimization that occurred and explains the event away as a "miscommunication" or "misunderstanding," meaning these survivors will not seek out the therapeutic support they need (Reed et al., 2020). Findings have shown that over 60% of rape survivors do not label their experience as rape and use only nonvictimizing terms to describe the event (Wilson & Miller, 2016). Reed and colleagues (2020) found in their study of 307 college students (35 men and 272 women) that 80% of the male participants and 51.1% of the female participants had unacknowledged rape experiences. These rates may vary among male identifying survivors, with heterosexual men being much less likely to endorse rape acknowledgment when compared to sexual minority men (Wilson & Newins, 2019). Unacknowledged rape has been associated with higher levels of psychopathology, decreased ability to utilize adaptive coping strategies, and greater life disability overall (Wilson et al., 2017).

High rates of RMA and unacknowledged rape have been consistently seen in both male and female survivors and are frequently endorsed by observers. Romero-Sanchez and colleagues (2018) conducted a study examining participants' views on various rape scenario vignettes to determine the impact substance use and acceptance of a drink from a male perpetrator had on participants' RMA. Over 88.6% of participants endorsed high levels of RMA and victim blaming when the survivor accepted and ingested an alcoholic beverage. They additionally found a strong positive correlation between RMA scores and scores on the measure of victim blame (Romero-Sanchez et al., 2018). Another study found that the rape myth of "men cannot be raped" was frequently endorsed by older male participants and these same participants also believed that males were more likely than females to make false reports to police regarding rape experiences (Walfield, 2018). Overall, higher rates of rape myth acceptance are likely to lead to increased assignment of self-blame to the survivor and decreased disclosure rates and treatment seeking behaviors (Lutz-Zois et al., 2015). In the general population, men tend to endorse higher rates of RMA compared to women. Angelone and colleagues (2020) found that this difference was due less to gender alone, but rather to sexist beliefs, gender stereotypes, or gender differentiation, as well as views on heterosexual intimacy that some men hold.

The biggest concern with RMA and unacknowledged rape is that it is highly likely to increase the level self-blame the survivor experiences, as well as decrease their willingness to disclose the nonconsensual sexual event(s), which does not allow them to obtain the services they need to support their recovery and address inaccurate self-blame beliefs (Reed et al., 2020). Wilson and colleagues (2017) conducted a study with 181 females who reported a history of rape since the age of 14. They proposed that individuals who acknowledged their own rape experiences but had high levels of RMA would be the group to report the highest levels of depression and significant substance abuse challenge. Their findings supported this hypothesis, which they believe is due to the women in this group experiencing higher rates of self-blame and attempting to make excuses for the perpetrator, allowing the blame to fall heavily on their own shoulders (Wilson et al., 2017). Lastly, Bernstein and colleagues (2022) found an indirect effect between RMA, PTSD symptoms, and self-blame, meaning RMA was positively associated with PTSD symptoms, which was then positively associated with self-blame.

Tonic Immobility (TI)

Tonic immobility (TI) is a physiological response elicited by prolonged physical restraint and intense fear which can involve "catatonic-like immobility with muscular hyper- or hypo-tonicity, odd postures, suppression of vocalization, intermittent eye closure, and Parkinson-like tremors" (Abrams et al., 2009, p. 550). The TI response often involves complete physical immobility, muscle rigidity, sympathetic and parasympathetic responses, and unfocused eye-gaze or stare (Humphreys et al., 2010). Research has shown that fear on its own is not enough to elicit TI, and instead there must be some form of restraint (Humphreys et al., 2010). TI is a part of the same system as the fight-flight response and has often been considered synonymous with the freeze response but has been much less studied and talked about than the other two fear responses (Gallup & Rager, 1996). However, it is inaccurate to use TI and the freeze response interchangeably, as they involve vastly different physiological responses and behavioral patterns (Coxell & King, 2010).

TI has been most widely researched in animals and is labeled a "defensive reflex" (Marx et al., 2008). Within the animal realm, research has found that when faced with a predator or direct threat, animals progress through a series of defensive reflexes, starting with freeze, then moving to flight or escape, then fight and struggle, and if met with a lack of success, the animals then move into a TI state due to exhausting all other options (Marx et al., 2008). The TI state can last anywhere from a few seconds to many hours depending on the continued presence of threat and current circumstances (Gallup, 1977).

Within the realm of human research, similar defensive responses to those of animals, have been observed, with the common language of "scared stiff" or "frozen with fear" utilized (Marx et al., 2008). During these experiences of TI, individuals remain cognitively aware and alert but are completely unable to defend themselves from threat, speak out, or act protectively in any way (Bovin et al., 2014). Research with human subjects has shown that experiences of significant, intense, and prolonged fear along with the belief that escape is not possible, have evoked TI responses (Bovin et al., 2014). Most of these studies have been conducted utilizing some form of physical restraint, but more recently, researchers have become aware that the belief in the inescapability of the current fear inducing stimuli is equal to any form of physical restraint (Gallup, 1977; Gallup & Rager, 1996). Instances of TI have also been witnessed in individuals when they are exposed to a loud, unexpected sound, flash of light, or other strong external stimuli that cause a direct change in the individual's environment (Gallup, 1977).

TI has been most widely seen within the realm of sexual assault, with the rates being higher than in any other type of assault or abuse (Bados et al., 2008). Many survivors of rape or other forms of sexual assault have reported a complete inability to move, speak, or call out for help during their nonconsensual sexual event, a phenomenon which has been previously termed "rape-induced paralysis" (Heidt et al., 2005, p. 1157). Suarez and Gallup (1979) first made the connection between this rape-induced paralysis and the TI response seen in nonhuman animals.

The first study on TI in sexual assault victims was conducted by Galliano and colleagues (1993), and they found that over 37% of their total participants experience a complete TI state during their sexual assault and every individual who reported immobilization displayed significantly higher rates of self-blame when compared to individuals who did not report TI-like symptoms (Galliano et al., 1993). A study conducted more recently by Heidt and colleagues (2005) examined 80 females between the ages of 18 and 51 who had experienced some form of CSA and that 62.1% of individuals who reported experiencing attempted or completed rape also endorsed symptoms consistent with TI.

Much less research has been conducted on TI responses in male survivors of sexual assault, which may lead to a lack of understanding and awareness of how natural this response could be for men (Coxell & King, 2010). One study found that a large percentage of their male participants experienced behavioral responses consistent with TI during a sexual assault, with 63% of heterosexual men, 59% of homosexual men, and 58% of bisexual men reporting similar experiences (Hodge & Canter, 1998). At this time, researchers are unaware of whether male survivors who experience TI during sexual assault may have differing outcomes than women who experience TI during sexual assault, which could have important therapeutic implications (Coxell & King, 2010).

Although minimal information exists regarding possible gender differences in TI responses, in general, this phenomenon is consistently seen to lead to significant negative outcomes for survivors (Hagenaars & Hagenaars, 2020). TI has been shown to lead to an increased risk of developing PTSD symptoms, slower recovery from these symptoms, and increased rates of depression, anxiety, and peritraumatic dissociation (Buren & Weierich, 2015; Hagenaars & Hagenaars, 2020; Heidt et al., 2005). Individuals who experienced TI during their nonconsensual sexual event(s) showed lower rates of responsiveness to treatment even six months after the initial assault (Kalaf, et al., 2015). TI may also be a strong predictor of increased feelings of guilt, shame, and self-blame (Bovin et al., 2014). Additionally, experiences of TI have been seen to not only increase the severity of PTSD symptoms but also alter the presentation of these symptoms, with higher rates of dissociation for survivors who experienced TI compared to those who did not (Abrams et al., 2009). One study conducted by Buren and Weierich (2015) found that survivors who experienced TI displayed higher rates of negative beliefs about others and the world but found that TI was not necessarily a predictor of higher levels of self-blame. The authors attribute this finding to the use of a less well-established measure of self-blame. Overall, TI may play a significant role in the aftermath of a nonconsensual sexual event, which could have significant implications for treatment of survivors.

Disclosure

Disclosure rates for survivors of both ASA and CSA are alarmingly low, with over one out of three survivors never reporting their abuse to anyone (Broman-Fulks et al., 2007). Rates of disclosure vary across demographic factors such as gender, race, and sexual orientation, with women often disclosing more frequently than men, and individuals of color disclosing less frequently than White individuals (Easton et al., 2014; Slatton & Richard, 2020). According to research data, 33% of women and 74% of men never disclosed their nonconsensual sexual event(s) to anyone, and for those who did disclose, it was often not immediate and could be delayed anywhere from 5 to 21 years depending on multiple factors (Easton, 2012; Pratt, 2022; Ulman, 2003). One study found that CSA survivors' length of time between the nonconsensual sexual event and disclosure ranged from 0 to 63 years, with a mean of over 20 years (Easton,

2019). Numerous barriers exist for the disclosure of nonconsensual sexual events including the identity of the perpetrator, with disclosure rates being lower when the perpetrator lives in the home, whether the abuse remains ongoing, and the victim's relationship to the perpetrator, with lower rates for immediate family members (Smith, 2020). Disclosure is an important factor to consider in the realm of sexual victimization experiences because if survivors are unable to share about their experiences, they are much less likely to receive adequate social support, obtain appropriate mental health services, and feel a heavy burden of maintaining their secret (Littleton, 2010). One study found that out of a sample of 210 women, approximately 43% had never disclosed their nonconsensual sexual event(s) to anyone before completing the online anonymous survey, and out of the 67% who did disclose, many of them had negative responses to their disclosure (Pratt, 2022).

Various cultural factors may influence disclosure rates. For example, high levels of religiosity or strict religious beliefs may lead some survivors to feel increased guilt and shame about their nonconsensual sexual event(s) due to taboo or beliefs viewing sex out of wedlock as a religious sin, thus decreasing the likelihood of early disclosure (Zalcberg, 2017). Differences may also occur across racial and ethnic groups. One study found that Hispanic women experienced more prolonged abuse, waited much longer to disclose, and more often were victimized by family members when compared to their White peers, due to fears surrounding possible repercussions from family or community members (Shaw et al., 2001). Another study conducted found that only 1 out of every 15 Black women who experienced ASA would disclose their assault at any point throughout their lives, even though the rates of sexual abuse and assault area higher for Black women than White women (Slatton & Richard, 2020). These authors suggested that decreased disclosure rates are seen within the Black community due to years of systematic oppression because of their race, experiences of marginalization and rejection, and the general delegitimization of Black women as experiencing SV (Slatton & Richard, 2020).

For male survivors of SV, both in childhood and adulthood, additional barriers to disclose may exist, leading to even lower rates of disclosure than are seen with women (Smith, 2020). Research has shown that somewhere between 10% to 33% of sexually abused boys do not disclose their abuse, and oftentimes wait until far into their adult years to engage in their first disclosure (Easton et al., 2014). Disclosure rates may be even lower among sexual minority men (SMM) due to gender biases surrounding SV, heteronormative views, homophobic attitudes, and societal acceptance of rape myths (Jackson et al., 2017; Rumney, 2009). The delayed disclosure of sexually abused boys and men appears to be strongly related to social stigma surrounding masculinity norms, rape myths beliefs than men cannot experience sexual victimization, and homophobic beliefs surrounding victimization by another male (Pratt, 2022; Smith, 2020). A qualitative study conducted by Easton and colleagues (2014) found that two of the primary barriers to disclosure for male survivors of CSA were societal norms surrounding masculinity as well as a lack of therapeutic resources and other resources for male survivors. These participants expressed concern that only the abuse of women was being verbalized and recognized and thus they did not feel safe enough to seek out support (Easton et al., 2014).

Studies on disclosure both in cases of CSA and ASA have been inconclusive, with mixed results (Easton, 2019). Some studies show that early disclosure within one month of the incident of CSA may lower the risk for survivors developing PTSD and disclosure to mother figures may lead to better psychological adjustment in later life (Broman-Fulks et al., 2007). Other studies have found that early disclosure may lead to an exacerbation of mental health symptoms or be completely unrelated to any mental health outcomes (O'Leary et al., 2010; Ullman & Filipas,

2005). One study examined different disclosure patterns among four groups which included immediate, delayed, crisis, and on-going disclosure groups, and the relationship to depression, posttraumatic stress, and physical health outcomes (Ahrens et al., 2010). Findings indicated the delayed and crisis disclosure groups had the highest rates of negative outcomes. Easton (2019) conducted a study with 487 adult male survivors of CSA on disclosure rates and the impact on mental health in adulthood. This study found that disclosure within a year after the first experience of CSA (i.e., early disclosure), acted as a strong protective factor for mental distress (Easton, 2019). One important factor to consider is that delayed disclosure makes it more challenging for survivors to receive therapeutic interventions and appropriate support, which is likely to lead to negative psychopathology, increased shame, guilt, and stronger beliefs in their responsibility for the abuse (Goodman & Brown et al., 2003).

Similar to CSA, the disclosure findings for ASA have been equally inconsistent (Ullman, 2011). Some studies have found that disclosure of ASA had no impact on psychological well-being, traumatic stress, or any physical symptoms (Kearns et al., 2010). Whereas others have found that disclosure may be highly correlated with improved psychological and physical health and well-being (Jacques-Tiura et al., 2010). The argument often presented by researchers is that disclosure alone may not have any impact on psychological well-being, but instead, the benefit, or lack thereof, comes from factors surrounding the disclosure itself, which may include responses from others, relationship with the perpetrator, and other broad factors (Ullman et al., 2010). The strongest focus has been placed on the factor of social support, comparing supportive and unsupportive responses to survivors' disclosures, thus the effects of disclosure may be fully dependent on the social responses.

One of the largest barriers to nonconsensual sexual event(s) disclosure is the survivor's fear that they may not be believed or even be blamed for the assault, leading many survivors to miss out on the possible benefits of social support and positive disclosure responses (Ullman et al., 2010). Even within a therapeutic setting, with specially trained professionals, survivors may still be hesitant to disclose due to similar fears or previous experiences of rejection and disbelief (Jacques-Tiura et al., 2010). A possible benefit of positive disclosure experiences is a significant increase in social support which is likely to lead to improved self-worth, self-esteem, and feelings of acceptance (Littleton, 2010). A meta-analysis conducted by Dworkin and colleagues (2019) found that throughout the literature, positive reactions to survivors' disclosure ended up acting as a protective factor, whereas negative responses involving blaming, attempts at control, distraction, and treating survivors differently led to significantly worse psychopathology. Another study comparing the disclosure experiences of Black and White female survivors of ASA found that negative responses from others had a much larger impact on symptoms and well-being than positive responses, which was consistent with previous findings (Jacques-Tiura et al., 2010). This study also found higher rates of negative responses to disclosure in Black females when compared to their White counterparts, but no differences in the beneficial impacts of positive disclosure between the two groups (Jacques-Tiura et al., 2010). More recent studies have highlighted the possible benefits of more public, often anonymous disclosures which have been spurred by the #MeToo movement, which can lead to feelings of increased emotional support, connectedness, and act as an antidote to self-blame and shame (Gueta et al., 2020).

Substance Use

Over half of the number of total sexual assaults per year involve alcohol use before or during the nonconsensual sexual event, with some studies finding that over 72% of female survivors report intoxication at the time of the assault (Relyea & Ullman, 2015). Alcohol is the most commonly used substance in instances of drug facilitated sexual assault (DFSA; Olszewski, 2009). DFSA can be defined as any instance of sexual assault in which the victim is too intoxicated to provide true consent to engaging in any sexual activities (Olszewski, 2009). The highest rates of sexual assault while under the influence of substances and DFSA occurs between the age ranges of 16 to 26, typically on college campuses, with many studies showing White cis-gendered females as the most common victims, which could be related to heterogenous research samples (Reed et al., 2009). In one study of college students with a sample of 513 males and 684 females, 70% of both male and female participants who experienced sexual victimization were either drinking, using drugs, or ingesting both substances at the time of their assault (Reed et al., 2009). This study also found substance use rates were similar between both the perpetrator and the survivor. Research has shown that being under the influence of alcohol or other substances may put individuals, specifically women, at higher risk of being sexually victimized. This in no way places the blame on the victim's shoulders, but may lead to increased fear of disclosure, due to fear of the victim not being believed or being blamed for their assault (Lorenz & Ullman, 2016). Additionally, sexual assault while under the influence is most often committed by someone who is known to the survivor, which may further complicate aftereffects of the assault, including disclosure and psychological functioning (Lorenz & Ullman, 2016). Far fewer studies have been conducted on the effects of substance use before or during CSA or ASA for male survivors.

One of the most important factors to consider when discussing substance intoxication during a nonconsensual sexual event is whether it may impact the survivor's willingness to disclose or the likelihood of any legal actions being taken against the perpetrator, and how both of these factors may impact the well-being of the survivor (Relyea & Ullman, 2015). One study found that college-aged female survivors who were under the influence at the time of the assault and then reported to formal agencies (e.g., campus security and local police) were revictimized by the dismissive responses, lack of support, and victim blaming behaviors, which all led to increased self-blame and guilt (Mennicke et al., 2019). Survivors may be hesitant to disclose if they were under the influence due to societal beliefs that these survivors' chose to put themselves in an altered state of mind, which made them more vulnerable to assault and unable to provide accurate details about the event itself (Hammock & Richardson, 1997). Male survivors already have lower rates of disclosure when compared to female survivors, and the addition of substance intoxication may only further decrease the likelihood of these men disclosing their abuse (Sivagurunathan et al., 2019).

Various hypotheses have been posed regarding the impact of both alcohol and drug intoxication during sexual assault and how this may impact the development of PTSD symptoms and severity (Jaffe et al., 2018). Findings have been inconsistent, with some studies finding that substance intoxication may lead to more severe and chronic PTSD symptoms, whereas others have found it acts more as a protective factor (Gong et al., 2019). Alcohol has been the most readily studied substance of use, with more recent research exploring the impact of additional substances. One study compared assault severity and post-assault outcomes across individuals who ingested drugs, alcohol, or both substances before their sexual assault (O'Callaghan & Ullman, 2021). These researchers found that individuals who ingested drugs only reported the most severe violence during the assault and had the worst mental health outcomes after the fact, but some findings may have been related to demographic factors, since the drug only group had the highest number of Black participants, who already report higher levels of violence and force during nonconsensual sexual events (O'Callaghan & Ullman, 2021).

Most researchers focus on the memory encoding processes as an explanation for how substance intoxication may impact specific symptoms of PTSD. For example, research has shown that alcohol intoxication negatively impacts episodic memory recall, or memories related to specific events (Soderlund et al., 2005). A study conducted by Jaffe and colleagues (2018) proposed that alcohol intoxication at the time of a traumatic event would increase the severity of re-experiencing symptoms due to episodic memory being heavily impacted, with semantic memories, specifically those that are affective in nature (e.g., smells, sounds, etc.), remaining intact. Their findings supported the hypotheses that survivors who were intoxicated before and/or during the nonconsensual sexual event were more likely to endorse PTSD symptoms. These authors argue that because contextual memories are less likely to be formed, the sensory memories become much more salient, leading to any sensory memory cue triggering a trauma response and re-experiencing episode for the survivor (Jaffe et al., 2018). Gong and colleagues (2019) had slightly different findings, their results indicated that substance intoxication at the time of the sexual assault resulted in fewer PTSD symptoms, but these symptoms were more chronic and often treatment resistant. Another theory related to the impact of substance intoxication during sexual assault is that because substances may dampen the stress-response, there is the potential for survivors to experience less symptom severity and for the substances to act as a protective factor (Levenson et al., 1980). Findings for this hypothesis have been varied, with some studies finding that substances do indeed decrease the stress response and others finding that they do not (Sher et al., 2007).

Sexual Arousal

Research has shown that physiological sexual arousal can and often does occur during periods of intense emotional arousal, even if the emotion is not related to love or lust (Dutton & Aron, 1974). Physiological arousal can be described as the bodily processes which occur during sexual arousal, including increased genital blood flow, swelling of various sex organs including the vagina, clitoris, and penis, increased genital sensation, and vaginal lubrication or penile erection (Masters & Johnson, 1966). Although many researchers have argued that the only way to assess physiological sexual arousal is through objective measures which pick up on actual physical cues (e.g., genital warmth, vaginal wall contraction, etc.), research has indicated that subjective reports of sexual arousal match up well and are highly correlated with the physiological measurements (Heinman, 1977; Mosher et al., 1988).

For women specifically, newer research has shown that sexual arousal may be strongly tied to activation of the sympathetic nervous system (SNS), which also plays a role in anxiety or fear responses (Lorenz et al., 2012). Some research has focused solely on SNS activation, with findings indicating that moderate levels of SNS activation led to increased genital arousal, whereas high levels of SNS activation led to decreased arousal (Bradford & Meston, 2006). Female sexual arousal is a complex process, with research findings connecting sexual arousal not only with activation of the SNS but also the parasympathetic nervous system (PNS) and peripheral nervous systems, indicating that the entire autonomic nervous system (ANS) may come into play to create physiological sexual arousal (Giuliano et al., 1995; Lorenz et al., 2012). It should be noted that physiological sexual arousal is differentiated from psychological sexual arousal, with physiological arousal being tied to the body's physical reactions and psychological arousal being tied to the emotional experiences such as pleasure, sexual interest, anticipation, and enjoyment (Bunderson, 2019; Hoon et al., 1977). Although these two experiences are often closely related, they are not dependent on one another and may act independently of each another (Paterson et al., 2014).

Some researchers have found that women's physiological sexual arousal tends to be less discriminatory, reacting to materials or activity that are not necessarily preferred, whereas male physiological sexual arousal tends to be discriminatory, reacting to only preferred material (Suschinsky & Lalumiere, 2011). Other findings have indicated that nonconsensual sexual stimulation, which occurs in CSA and ASA, can lead to physiological arousal and even orgasm in both men and women (Gilmore et al., 2010; Levin & van Berlo, 2004). Epinephrine and norepinephrine have been identified as playing a role in physiological sexual arousal, and both of these neurotransmitters are known to play a strong role in fear and anxiety responses (Bunderson, 2019). This means an individual who experiences a high level of fear or anxiety may also experience a similarly high level of physiological sexual arousal, even though there are not any specific stimuli that would elicit a psychological sexual arousal (Lorenz et al., 2012). This link between high levels of fear and sexual arousal was supported by Dutton and Aron (1974) who found a strong correlation between women's self-reported level of fear and self-report level of sexual arousal. Arguments have also been made for the fact that women's physiological sexual arousal, which causes lubrication of the vagina, may be a natural protective or preparatory bodily response to avoid harm or damage to the vaginal walls, which would strongly tie this physical response to situations which induce fear or anxiety; known as the Preparation Hypothesis (Suschinsky & Lalumiere, 2011).

Research has also found that increased anxiety, fear of being punished, panic attacks and high levels of other emotional states may be associated with both premature, unexpected, and/or spontaneous ejaculation in males (Fuchs, 2004; Redmond et al., 1983). Additionally, for men, anal penetration is highly likely to lead to psychological sexual arousal and ejaculation even during periods of nonconsensual sexual activity (Bullock & Beckson, 2011). Research has shown that in these instances, this response is completely biological and reflexive in nature and is not indicative of the survivor experiencing any type of desire, interest, or pleasure (Bunderson, 2019). It should be noted that many rapes committed against men involve anal penetration, either with foreign objects (including fingers) or penises (McLean, 2013). If survivors experience sexual arousal or orgasm during their nonconsensual sexual event, it is likely to lead to increased feelings of shame, self-blame, and confusion regarding the experience (Bunderson, 2019). Survivors may be confused by their bodily responses and question the nature of their experience, increasing the likelihood of unacknowledged rape and delayed disclosure (Romero-Sanchez et a., 2018). Perpetrators may also use victims' sexual arousal or orgasm as evidentiary support for the consensual nature of the assault, thus eliciting further power and control over the survivor (Bullock & Beckson, 2011). Lastly, when survivors experience sexual arousal and/or orgasm, they are much less likely to report their assault to law enforcement agencies due to fears surrounding the possibility of these details being brought up during an investigation (Bunderson, 2019). It is important that clinicians are aware of these possible responses to sexual assault and focus on normalizing and discussing these reactions with clients, rather than waiting for them to bring these concerns up on their own, which they are unlikely to do. Additionally, there are important implications for how policy and practice identify and distinguish between consent, arousal, pleasure, and how these factors play out in nonconsensual encounters (Yun & Michael, 2021).

Purpose of the Study

The purpose of this research was to explore the relationship between various characteristics of nonconsensual sexual experiences, both ASA and CSA, and how these factors may predict the severity of trauma-related self-blame in male survivors. Specifically, this research explored whether male survivors who experienced TI or sexual arousal or substance use during the nonconsensual experience, or had unsupportive disclosure responses afterward, or endorse rape myth acceptance, reported higher rates of trauma-related self-blame when compared to survivors who did not have these experiences.

Research Questions and Hypotheses

Research Question 1. Is there a significant relationship between the number of nonconsensual sexual event categories experienced, including both CSA and ASA, and trauma-related self-blame?

Hypothesis 1. The number of nonconsensual sexual event categories experienced in both childhood and adulthood, as measured by the Sexual Experiences Survey, will be positively correlated with self-blame, as measured by the Rape Attribution Questionnaire (RAQ).

Research Question 2. For men, is there a relationship between RMA and trauma-related self-blame?

Hypothesis 2. Levels of RMA reported by male survivors, as measured by the Gender-Inclusive Rape Myth Acceptance Scale (GIIRMA), will be positively correlated with levels of self-blame, as measured by the Rape Attribution Questionnaire (RAQ).

Research Question 3. Is there a significant relationship between the level of TI experienced during a nonconsensual sexual event and trauma-related self-blame for men?

Hypothesis 3. Men who experienced higher levels of TI during the assault, as measured by the Tonic Immobility Scale (TIS), will be positively correlated with greater self-blame, as measured by the Rape Attribution Questionnaire (RAQ).

Research Question 4a. Is there a relationship between men's disclosure of a nonconsensual sexual experience and trauma-related self-blame?

Hypothesis 4a. Male survivors who have disclosed their nonconsensual sexual event will have significantly lower self-blame, as measured by the Rape Attribution Questionnaire (RAQ), than individuals who have not disclosed.

Research Question 4b. Is there a relationship between the supportiveness of a response to disclosure of a nonconsensual sexual event and trauma-related self-blame for men?

Hypothesis 4b. More unsupportive disclosure responses, as measured by the Checklist of Abuse and Related Stressors (C-SARS), will be positively correlated with greater self-blame for men, as measured by the Rape Attribution Questionnaire (RAQ).

Research Question 5. For men, is there a relationship between the consumption of substances before the occurrence of a nonconsensual sexual event and trauma-related self-blame?

Hypothesis 5. Male survivors who voluntarily consumed any drugs or alcohol prior to the CSA or ASA incident will endorse significantly higher levels of self-blame, as measured by the Rape Attribution Questionnaire (RAQ).

Research Question 6. For men, is there a relationship between sexual arousal experienced during a nonconsensual sexual event and trauma-related self-blame?

Hypothesis 6. Male survivors who endorse experiencing sexual arousal during sexual assault, as measured by the Subjective Sexual Arousal Rating Scale, will report higher levels of self-blame, as measured by the Rape Attribution Questionnaire (RAQ).

Clinical and Theoretical Relevance

The goal of this research was to expand the ASA and CSA literature for male survivors, specifically exploring factors related to the development of self-blame. This research has the potential to provide important information to all treatment providers working with male survivors of SV about the unique factors which may contribute to worse or treatment-resistant symptoms. It is imperative for clinicians to be aware of how impactful experiences such as TI, sexual arousal, substance intoxication, and RMA may be on survivors. These are not topics that therapists or psychologists are trained in, and with increased awareness of these topics mental health providers can address these experiences early on with survivors. That could lead to earlier and greater improvements in therapeutic outcomes. Additionally, initiating a discussion of these topics, whether or not the client discloses them, can provide the opportunity for clinicians to normalize these symptoms and experiences, thus providing comfort for the survivors and possibly increasing the likelihood of disclosure. The methods and results of this study have the potential to increase the knowledge base of experiences which are common across many survivors.

Chapter II

Methods

Research Design

This study aimed identify what factors may predict higher levels of trauma-related self-blame in survivors of ASA or CSA. Predictor variables included sexual assault history, experiences of TI, disclosure experiences, use of substances before or during the event, sexual arousal during the nonconsensual sexual event, and agreement with various rape myths. A quantitative analysis was conducted to determine the strength of the different predictors. A major goal of this study was to make it generalizable across other individuals who have had these experiences, and thus a survey method was used to meet this goal (Anderson et al., 2013). Previous research has shown that although online surveys may lead to exclusion of non-internet users, they are still a reliable and valid means of collecting data and are likely to still include a diverse sample (Deutskens et al., 2006).

This survey was titled, Personal Experiences Related to Nonconsensual Sexual Events, and was designed on Qualtrics. Men who experienced sexual assault in adulthood, sexual abuse in childhood, or both events were included in the study. For the purposes of this study, CSA was defined using the Center for Disease Control and Prevention (CDC) and The World Health Organization (WHO) definitions of this phenomenon which state, "any completed or attempted (noncompleted) sexual act, sexual contact with, or exploitation of a child, (Leeb et al., 2008) and an activity between a child and an adult, which can include unlawful sexual activity, practices, or exploitation of pornographic materials. These sexual activities must occur before the age of 14 and may include contact activities such as fondling or intercourse of any kind (Leeb et al., 2008). ASA was defined as any sexual contact that occurs without direct consent including attempted rape, fondling or unwanted touch, penetration of any form, and, or forcing the individual to perform any type of sexual act (RAINN, 2019). All survey data collection occurred at a single time point and did not require participants to return to complete additional survey components. All items on the survey were combination of yes/no responses, multiple choice options, and Likert-type scale responses. Predictor variables were number of CSA and ASA events, TI experiences, disclosure, substance consumption, sexual arousal, and rape myth acceptance. Outcome variables for each hypothesis were levels of trauma-related self-blame.

Participants

To participate in this study individuals had to meet the following criteria: (a) 18 years of age or older, (b) cisgender male; assigned male at birth and currently identifies as a male, (c) experienced some form of a nonconsensual sexual event during their lifespan, (d) have access to the internet (to complete the online survey), (e) self-reported English fluency (because all assessment measures, consent forms, and resources are in English), (f) currently a resident of the United States. A nonconsensual sexual event was defined as: any sexual act occurring within the life span and could include actions such as fondling, unwanted sexual touching, or intercourse of any kind (including vaginal, oral, and anal), forced viewing or showing of genitals, being forced to view or perform sexual acts, child pornography, sex trafficking, attempted rape, and/or any other sexual conduct. There were no additional exclusion criteria.

Protection of Human Participants

Ethics Codes laid out by both the American Psychological Association (APA) and the Institutional Review Board of Alliant International University (AIU) were abided by in the design of this study (APA, 2017). Before beginning the study, participants completed a participation criteria screener which required them to confirm whether they met all required criteria. If participants were removed from the study during the screener, they were automatically redirected to a page with resources they could download and utilize, including emergency hotline numbers, peer support groups, literature, and ways to connect with mental health professionals. After completing the screener, participants were provided a digital consent form which they could also download and keep for their records. The Informed Consent (Appendix A) document contained information regarding a brief summary of the purpose of the study and individual's rights and abilities within their participation in this study. The mental health resources were also included in the Informed Consent form.

Participants were then required to provide their consent to participate in the study or to leave the study immediately by checking "yes, I confirm I meet the aforementioned criteria and agree to participate in this study" or "no, I do not wish to participate in this study." Risk of participating in this study was minimal and participants were given the option to terminate the study up until the debriefing form, where they could select to submit their responses, or terminate their responses. This study was conducted online via an anonymous Qualtrics survey. Participants were not asked to provide any identifying information in the survey and all survey data has been stored on a password-protected computer, which only the Principal Investigator (PI) has access to. All data will be kept for a period of seven years after the completion of the study, per the Alliant International University's IRB requirements.

Instrumentation

After participants were screened for inclusion criteria, they were asked to complete a standard Demographic Questionnaire (Appendix B) along with six questionnaires: Sexual Experience – Short Form – Victim (SES-SFV; Appendix C), Rape Attribution Questionnaire (RAQ; Appendix D), Gender-Inclusive Illinois Rape Myth Acceptance Scale (GIIRMA;

Appendix E), Tonic Immobility Scale (TIS; Appendix F), Checklist of Sexual Abuse and Related Stressors (CSARS; Appendix G), and Subjective Sexual Arousal Rating Scale (Appendix H). Participants had access to all five measures via the Qualtrics survey. This survey was piloted by 5-10 graduate students before the survey was published for research participants to determine how long it takes to complete the study. Findings indicated an average time of 12-15 minutes when thoroughly reading the Informed Consent and Resources documents, with an average time of 8-10 minutes for individuals who only thoroughly read questions and answers.

Demographic Questionnaire

A Demographic Questionnaire (Appendix B) was developed by the PI, which contains questions relevant to this specific area of research. Questions asked participants about their age, gender, ethnicity, race, and sexual orientation. Participants were also asked about their experiences of sexual assault in adulthood and/or sexual abuse in childhood and whether they consumed any substances 12 hours or less before their experience(s) of nonconsensual sex. The Demographics Questionnaire (Appendix B) consisted of ten questions total. The purpose of this questionnaire was to obtain individual characteristics of the participants which may be relevant for determining between-group differences and adds to a better understanding of the unique within-group differences. Additionally, this questionnaire serves a way to assess for substance use both prior to and, or during the nonconsensual act, with is relevant to the hypotheses of this study.

Sexual Experiences – Short Form – Victimization (SES-SFV)

The original items for the Sexual Experiences Survey (SES) were developed in 1982 by Koss and Gidycz, and the survey was tested for validity and reliability in 1985 (Koss & Oros, 1985). The original measure was developed due to concerns with the lack of sexual assaults being reported and a call for intensive research on this topic (Koss & Gidycz, 1985). This measure was developed as a combined victim and perpetrator assessment, with assumptions in the measure that males were the primary perpetrators and females the primary victims, including gender specific language and heteronormative assumptions (Littleton et al., 2018). A few years later the Sexual Experiences – Short Form (SES-SF) and Long Form (SES-LF) versions were developed because of concerns with validity and reliability of the original measure (Anderson et al., 2018). These new versions of the assessment had separate measures for victims and perpetrators and eliminated the gendered language and heteronormative biases (Littleton et al., 2018). Sexual Experience – Short Form – Victimization (SES-SFV) and Sexual Experiences – Long Form – Victimization (SES-LFV) have often been considered the gold standard within the field to measure sexual victimization (Anderson et al., 2018).

The SES-SFV (Appendix C) is a self-report assessment established to measure sexual victimization and the severity of these experiences (Koss & Gidycz, 1985). The SES-SFV consists of nine questions related to different nonconsensual sexual experiences including "someone had oral sex with me or made me have oral sex with them without my consent" and "someone fondled, kissed, or rubbed up against the private areas of my body (Anderson et al., 2018). Two of the sexual experiences' questions consist of female specific sexual experiences involving vaginal penetration, which are removed from the survey when it is being used with males (Littleton et al., 2018).

Each of the seven questions then have the same A through E questions which relate to different types of coercion or force that may have been used by the perpetrator, before, during, or after the experiences (Littleton et al., 2018). For example, question two states "someone had oral sex with me or made me have oral sex with them without my consent by:" and then asks the respondent to answer questions A through E related to this specific experience. Questions A through E include: "threatening to physically harm me or someone close to me" and "using force, for example, holding me down with their body weight, pinning my arms, or having a weapon." Due to IRB concerns with the sensitive nature of some of these questions, the were removed from the final survey to allow for increased likelihood that participants would be comfortable completing the survey. In the original survey, participants are also asked to rate the number of times each sexual event has occurred, as well as the number of times each type of coercion or control was used, ranging from 0 times to 3+. Participants are asked to rate all these items based on how many times the experiences have occurred in the last 12 months, how many times they occurred before the age of 14, and how many times they occurred after the age of 14 (Koss & Gidycz, 1985). IRB requested that changes also be made to this portion of the survey, allowing participants to answer with yes/no rather than specifying the number of times each event occurred. For the final survey, answer choices were adjusted to "Yes, ONLY before the age of 14," "Yes, ONLY after the age of 14," "Yes, BOTH before and after the age of 14," and "this has not happened to me." Internal consistency for the SES-SFV is .92 for females and .98 for males and when compared to the original, longer version, the SES, the SES-SFV was significantly correlated at $r = .52$, $p < .01$ (Johnson et al., 2017). Although adjustments were made to the ratings of the question items, this test remains a strong measure of SV experiences.

Rape Attribution Questionnaire (RAQ)

The RAQ (Appendix D) is a 25-item, self-report measure rated on both a 5-point Likert type scale with answer choices ranging from Never (1) to Very Often (5) and choices ranging from Strongly Disagree (1) to Strongly Agree (5; Frazier, 2003). This measure was designed to assess for survivors' beliefs about why a nonconsensual sexual activity occurred, who is responsible, how this event has impacted their future, and what control they believe they have over the healing process (Frazier, 2003). The total scale consists of five subscales including Characterological Self-Blame, Behavioral Self-Blame, Rapist Blame, Control Over the Recovery Process, Future Likelihood, and Future Control (Fazier, 2003). Additionally, this measure assesses three aspects of control, including present control, future control, and perceived control over future assaults (Frazier, 2003).

This measure starts with a prompt which states: "how often have you had the thought: I was assaulted because…?" which is followed by the Likert-type questions. For the purposes of this study, only the five Characterological Self-Blame items and the Behavioral Self-Blame items will be used, to create a specific measure of survivors' self-blame. Questions include things like, "this happens to people like me," and "I used poor judgement" (Frazier, 2008). Scores from these 10 items will be added to create a total self-blame score, with scores ranging from 10-100. Higher scores on this measure are indicative of higher rates of self-blame due to the nonconsensual sexual activity. Overall reliability of the scale is strong with a Cronbach's alpha of .83 and test-retest reliability at .68 to .80 for female survivors of sexual assault (Bhuptani & Messman, 2021; Sigurvinsdottir & Ullman, 2015; Ullman et al., 2014). Although this scale has been much less extensively used with male survivors, reliability rates remain appropriate in the range of .57 to .71 (Mallett, 2014). And of most importance to this study, individual subscale alpha coefficients range from .77 to .89 (Bhuptani & Messman, 2021; Frazier, 2003; Sigurvinsdottir & Ullman, 2015).

Gender-Inclusive Illinois Rape Myth Acceptance Scale (GIIRMA)

The Illinois Rape Myth Acceptance Scale (IRMAS) is self-report measure designed to assess for belief and alignment with prejudicial, stereotypical, and false beliefs about rape, rape victims, and rapists (Payne et al., 1999). The original scale consists of 45 questions which are all answered on a 7-point Likert-type scale ranging from Not at all Agree (1) to Very Much Agree (7). There are seven subscales which each directly relate to well-known rape myths include, (1) She Wanted It, (2) She Asked for It, (3) She Lied, (4) It Wasn't Really Rape, (5) He Didn't Mean to, (6) Rape is a Trivial Event, and (7) Rape is a Deviant Event (Payne et al., 1999). Higher scores on this measure indicate a higher level of RMA. Scores are totaled by adding up the rating for each item that loads onto a specific subscale, and then adding these items together for a total scale score. Because of concerns regarding biased responding the authors included filler items with negative wording which are not included in the total score calculations (Payne et al., 1999). This measure has shown strong reliability and validity. Reliability for the total score, a combination of all the subscales, is $\alpha = .93$ and the subscale total scores range from $\alpha = .74$ to .84 (Payne et al., 1999; Johnson et al., 2021). Test-retest reliability has been shown at .90 and has shown convergent validity related to violence and sexist beliefs (Kikue & Diem, 2000; Payne et al., 1999). The IRMA is one of the best known and most frequently used measures to assess for RMA. It has been used with various populations including perpetrators, survivors, college students, police, military personnel, individuals connected with religious organizations, and many others (Suarez & Gadalla, 2010; Lonsway & Fitzgerald, 1994).

A modified version of this measure was created by McMahon and Farmer (2011), which removed filler items, shorted the measure substantially, changed the Likert scale, and adjusted the subscales down to five total scales which were more aligned with updated research on RMA. The modified version was shortened to 18 items with the new Likert-type scale ranging from Strongly Disagree (1) to Strongly Agree (5). Lower scores are now indicative of higher RMA. The Likert-type scale was adjusted to address the negatively worded filler questions on the previous version, so rather than including the filler items, and lengthening the measure, the authors opted for a shorter measure with an adjusted Likert scale (McMahon & Farmer, 2011). The five subscales included in the updated version are: (1) She Asked for It, (2) He Didn't Mean To, (3) He Didn't Mean To (Intoxication), (4) It was not Really Rape, and (5) She Lied (McMahon & Farmer, 2011). The modified version has been shown to have very similar reliability and validity to the original version (Johnson et al., 2012).

Due to the gender stereotyped language of the original IRMA as well as the modified version, which both focus exclusively on females being the victims of rape and men being the perpetrators, an updated, gender-inclusive version of the modified measure will be utilized for this study, the Gender-Inclusive Illinois Rape Myth Acceptance Scale (GIIRMA; Johnson et al., 2021; Appendix E). The modified measure questions included items such as "if a girl is raped while she's drunk, she is at least somewhat responsible for letting it get out of control" and "rape happens when a man's sex drive gets out of control" (Payne et al., 1999). In the new version of this scale, the five subscales remain the same as the modified version of the IRMA, but the gendered language has been changed, so rather than subscale one stating, "She Asked for It" it now reads "The Victim Asked for It" (Johnson et al., 2021). Individual items were also adjusted to encompass the gender-neutral language. For example, the original item stated, "if a girl is raped while she's drunk, she is at least somewhat responsible for letting things get out of control" the new item now states, "if someone is raped while they are drunk, they are at least somewhat responsible for letting things get out of hand" (Johnson et al., 2021). Scores at and above 45 are considered significant (Johnson et al., 2021). This measure has been normed on a diverse population of various sexual orientations and gender identities. Statistical findings indicated excellent internal consistency of $\alpha = .97$, with the five factors ranging from $\alpha = .82$-.92

(Johnson et al., 2021). For gender diverse individuals, internal consistency remained at .97, with comparability across gender identifications and sexual orientations (Johnson et al., 2021). For the purposes of this study, a question has been added to this assessment, "men cannot be raped" to determine how this specific rape myth may impact experiences of self-blame.

Tonic Immobility Scale (TIS)

The TIS (Appendix F) is a scale designed to measure the presence and severity of multiple features of TI in survivors of sexual assault (Forsyth et al., 2000). It was initially developed for use with female survivors but has been expanded for use with male survivors as well (Kalaf et al., 2017). The TIS has a two-factor structure assessing both TI bodily responses and Fear experiences (Covers et al., 2021). Internal consistency for the TI factor was .94 and .90 for the Fear factor (Fuse et al., 2007). The measure is split into two sections, with the first section consisting of 10-items asking about the core components of TI related to the most recent nonconsensual sexual activity, and the second 10 items asking about the same experiences across the lifetime (Moller et al., 2017).

The first 10 questions of this measure are rated a 7-point Likert-type scale ranging from zero to six. These items are added together with scores ranging from 0 to 60 and higher scores on this portion of the measure indicating higher TI behaviors and Fear experiences during the any of their previous sexual assault experiences (Fuse et al., 2007). Seven questions are related to immobility experiences and three are related to fear experiences. Question 11 is not included in the total score and instead is intended as a means of obtaining data related to additional incidents of assault or abuse outside of the most recent incident reported. The first 10 questions include "Rate the degree to which you were unable to call our or scream during the event" and "Rate the extent to which you felt detached from yourself during the event" (Forsyth et al., 2000). Scores of 21 or above are indicative of significant experiences of immobility and scores of 9 or greater are indicative of significant fear (Heidt et al., 2005). Significant immobility is defined as a score of 21 or greater and significant fear is defined as a score of 9 or greater (Heidt et al., 2005). The second portion of the assessment asks about the same 10 core symptoms in part one of the assessment but related to any other experiences of nonconsensual sexual activity, rather than just the most recent experience (Heidt et al., 2005). The last 10 questions are answered with "yes" or "no" responses and are not included in the total score, but rather are used as qualitative information related to lifetime experiences of these symptoms (Fuse et al., 2007). Cronbach's for the entire scale is 0.87; 0.81 for the TI subscale and 0.62 for the Fear subscale (Moller et al., 2017).

Checklist of Sexual Abuse and Related Stressors (C-SARS)

The C-SARS (Appendix G) was developed as a 70-item measure to assess for negative and stressful life events related to sexual abuse experiences (Spaccarelli, 1995). This measure assesses for three separate types of stressful events, abuse-specific events, abuse-related events, and public disclosure events, all directly related to sexual abuse by one specific perpetrator (Spaccarelli & Fuchs, 1997; Strand et al., 2005). Questions are answered dichotomously with a "yes" or "no" response. For this study, only the 7-items from the Negative Disclosure Experiences subscale will be utilized, and only participants who endorsed previously disclosing their abuse will be asked to complete this measure. These 7-items include questions such as: "some of your family or friends scolded you or punished you when they found out what happened" and "some of your family or friends were angry at you when they found out what happened" (Spaccarelli & Fuchs, 1997). This scale will be used specifically to measure stressors participants experienced directly related to them disclosing their abuse to someone. Total scores will be calculated by adding up the number of "yes" responses endorsed; thus, scores range from zero to seven, with higher scores indicating the presence of more unsupportive responses during disclosure experiences (Strand et al., 2005).

Multiple studies have confirmed the C-SARS (Appendix G) as a valid and reliable measure of sexual abuse related stressors for survivors of sexual abuse and sexual assault (Spaccarelli & Fuchs, 1997; Strand et al., 2005; Wilczynski et al., 2015). For the entire scale, internal consistency has ranged from Cronbach's alphas of .71 to .93 (Johnson & Young, 2007; Pratt, 2022; Spaccarelli, 1995). Additionally, construct validity has had conflicting results with some authors reporting poor validity due to lack of support between this measure and therapist reports of behavior problems and stress, whereas other authors report the opposite (Strand et al., 2005; Wilczynski et al., 2015). Concurrent validity for this scale has been primarily poor due to the lack of association with symptoms such as depression and anxiety, which is very common among many widely used abuse screening tools (Strand et al., 2005; Wilczynski et al., 2015). This indicates that results should be interpreted alongside further assessment measures and additional supporting evidence. This measure has also shown moderate convergent validity with the Negative Appraisals of Sexual Abuse Scale (NASAS; $r = .34$), which measures individuals' negative cognitive appraisals of their own sexual abuse experiences, specifically related to threat, harm, or loss, as a result of this abuse (Spaccarelli, 1995). Most important to this study, the Public Disclosure Events subscale has good internal consistency at $\alpha = .70$ (Spaccarelli, 1995; Spaccarelli & Fuchs, 1997).

Subjective Sexual Arousal Rating Scale

The Subjective Sexual Arousal Rating (Appendix H) scale is a 7-item measure that utilizes a 7-point Likert-type scale and self-report method, which was originally developed in

1980 (Mosher & White, 1980). The Likert-type scale ranges from Did Not Experience This at All (1) to Experienced This to an Extreme Degree (7) and participants are asked to choose the answer that best represents how they felt during their sexual event (Mosher et al., 2010). Scores on this measure range from 7 to 49, with higher scores indicating more feelings, sensations, and bodily experiences related to sexual arousal and scores at and above 35 being considered significant (Mosher et al., 2010). This measure was originally designed for use with female college students to assess for physiological sexual arousal and sexual affects by asking questions related to muscular tension, non-genital physical sensations, genital sensations, and sexual warmth, and was then expanded for use with male participants as well (Mosher et al., 2010; Mosher & White, 1980). Each item contains a brief description of the experience participants are being asked to rate, which includes "Sexual Absorption – a subjective estimate of your level of absorption in the sensory components of the experience," "Sexual Arousal – a subjective estimate of your overall level of sexual arousal," and "Sexual interest – a subjective estimate of your degree of present interest in sexual imagery or activities" (Mosher et al., 2010). Slight modifications will be made to the measure to remove the female focused language from item number 3, Sexual Warmth, which discusses "sexual warmth experienced in the breasts" (Mosher et al., 2010). Cronbach's alpha for this measure ranged from .95 to .97, with significant validity coefficients for male participants ranging from .15 to .81 with a median of .56 (Mosher et al., 2010).

Procedures

Recruitment.

The current study required a total of 200 participants as estimated using G*Power 3.1 and effect sizes from similar previous studies. Participants were recruited through the MTurk survey platform, which involves offering small monetary reward for participants to complete an online survey (Cheung et al., 2017). MTurk is a "crowdsourcing marketplace that makes it easier for individuals and businesses…to conduct simple data validation and research more subjective tasks like survey participation…and augment data collection and analysis… (MTurk, 2022-a) The platform recommends paying approximately 10 cents per minute of time expected for completion of the survey (MTurk, 2022-b). Due to pilot testing of the survey estimating an average of 15 minutes for completion time, participants were offered $1.50 for completion of the survey. Participants accessed the survey through the MTurk platform where the Qualtrics survey was linked. At the end of the survey participants were required to obtain an individual ID number to prove they had thoughtfully completed the entire survey.

Research regarding the use of online panels for data collection such as Qualtrics, SurveyMonkey, and Mechanical Turk (MTurk) has been growing over the past few years. Use of these online platforms has advantages over traditional recruitment methods in that a more representative, nation-wide sample can be obtained, which is more challenging to do with traditional paper-based survey methods (Lowry et al., 2016). When using a panel or online recruitment platform for recruitment, additional precautionary methods are included in data collection such as IP verification, removal of bots, and duplication prevention, which can improve the quality of survey data collected (Miller et al., 2020). Although there can be methodological concerns with MTurk data, these concerns can be remedied through the use of additional validity inferences as recommended by Cheung and colleagues (2017), which were used for this study and discussed in detail in Chapter III. There is growing research supporting the use of online platforms for research recruitment procedures and the utilization of these methods has been well received with the social sciences and other behavioral research projects

(Eyal et al., 2021). MTurk has been found to be one of the most demographically and politically representative recruitment methods when compared to other methods (Boas et al., 2018).

A recruitment flyer was distributed to through the MTurk platform which stated: *We are interested in understanding your experience as a survivor of a nonconsensual sexual event, rape, abuse, sexual assault, SV, and/or sexual victimization at some point in my lifetime. These acts can be defined as any sexual act occurring within the life span and could include actions such as fondling, unwanted sexual touching, or intercourse of any kind (including vaginal, oral, and anal), forced viewing or showing of genitals, being forced to view or perform sexual acts, child pornography, sex trafficking, attempted rape, and/or any other sexual conduct, in which consent is not freely given. It is our goal to bring to light unique experiences so that others who have had similar experiences recognize that they are not alone. Your participation will help provide important information and contribute to enhanced treatment services for other survivors.*

Online Procedures.

The recruitment advertisement contained the Qualtrics survey link which directed individuals to click on the URL to begin their participation in the study. Participants first completed the inclusion and exclusion screener section of the survey, which required a singular yes/no response, and required participants to choose a response before continuing. These questions asked participants about whether they were: 18 years of age or older, identify as a cis-gender male, are a resident of the United States, are a survivor of SV, and at least four months have passed since their most recent nonconsensual sexual event. If participants did not meet all of the inclusion criteria they were immediately removed from the study and redirected to a screen which included a brief thank you for them attempting to participate in the study and offering their time, a short debriefing form, and mental health resources and emergency hotline numbers. After completion of the participation screener participants were provided the Informed Consent document and a list of mental health resources. Participants were asked to click "yes, I consent to participate in this study," before moving on to the next portion of the survey. Once consent was given, participants were then directed to the Demographic Questionnaire, which included a nonconsensual sexual event screener.

After completion of the Demographic Questionnaire, participants were directed to complete the SES-SFV to assess for CSA and ASA history. Next, participants were directed to complete the TSI to measure TI symptoms and fear experienced during the nonconsensual sexual event, a yes/no question asking if they have previously disclosed their assault or abuse to anyone, and the C-SARS to measure unsupportive disclosure responses. Participants were directed to the C-SARS if they answer "yes" for whether they have previously disclosed. Participants who answered "no" to this question were immediately directed to take the Subjective Sexual Arousal Rating Scale, which participants who endorsed "yes" completed as well, to assess whether the individual experienced sexual arousal during the nonconsensual sexual event. All participants were then directed to complete the RAQ to examine trauma-related self-blame experiences. After completing all these measures, participants were lastly directed to the completion page, which provided a short debrief, a list of mental health resources, and offered a brief thank you to participants for offering their time to complete the survey.

Data Analysis

SPSS, software version 28, was utilized to conduct all statistical analysis.

Analyses for hypothesis 1, 2, 3, 4b, and 6 were conducted utilizing a single multiple linear regression. This model assessed for the relationship between five independent variables (number of CSA and ASA events, rape myth acceptance, TI, unsupportive disclosure responses, and sexual arousal) and the dependent variable (trauma-related self-blame). Related studies indicated a Cohen's $d = 0.4$ and $R^2 = .10$ to .31 for effect sizes between sexual victimization history and self-blame (Pratt, 2020; Quas et al., 2003; Breitenbecher, 2006), an $R^2 = .20$ for rape myth acceptance and self-blame (Walfield, 2018), Cohen's $d = 0.5$ and $R^2 = .103$ effect sizes between TI and self-blame (Moller et al., 2017; Pratt, 2022), and a Cohen's $d = 0.4$ and $R^2 = 0.10$ to 0.26 effect sizes between unsupportive disclosure responses and self-blame (Littleton, 2010; Sigurvinsdottir & Ullman, 2014; Pratt, 2022; Ullman & Najdowski, 2011), and a Cohen's $d = 0.1$ and $R^2 = 0.10$ to 0.13 effect sizes between sexual arousal and self-blame (Bunderson, 2019; Fuchs, 2004; Hyun & Salter, 2021) Assessing the range of effect sizes from the various factors (Blayney et al., 2016; Breitenbecher, 2006; Bunderson, 2019; Filipas & Ullman, 2006; Fuchs, 2004; Hunter et al., 2012; Littleton, 2010; Moller et al., 2017; Pratt, 2022; Quas et al., 2003; Sigurvinsdottir & Ullman, 2014; Ullman & Najdowski, 2011; Walfield, 2018), an effect size of Cohen's $d = 0.42$, converted to $f^2 = 0.15$, and $R^2 = .23$, converted to $f^2 = 0.35$, with an average effect size of $f^2 = 0.25$ were indicated between self-blame and the combinations of factors: sexual history, rape myth acceptance, TI, disclosure, and sexual arousal. Due to many of these previous studies being conducted with women and the current study being conducted with men, a more conservative effect size of $f^2 = 0.20$ was deemed appropriate for this study. An a priori analysis was conducted using G*power 3.1 software to determine an approximate sample size needed to power the analysis (Faul et al., 2009). With a power of 0.80 and a two-tailed alpha level of 0.05, the estimated sample size needed to obtain a 0.20 effect size was 70 participants.

Hypothesis 4a was tested utilizing a two-tailed *t-test*. This model assessed for the relationship between disclosure and trauma-related self-blame. Related studies indicated effect sizes ranging from $d = 0.2$ to 0.6 and $\eta^2 = 0.05$ (Ahrens et al., 2010; Goodman-Brown et al.,

2003; Hunter et al., 2012); thus, a medium effect size of 0.4 was used. An a priori analysis was conducted using G*power 3.1 software to determine an approximate sample size needed to power the analysis (Faul et al., 2009). With a power of 0.80 and a two-tailed alpha level of 0.05, the estimated sample size needed to obtain a 0.4 effect size was 200, with at least 100 participants in each group, with groups separated by disclosure or nondisclosure.

Hypothesis 5 was tested utilizing a two-tailed *t-test.* This model assesses for the relationship between the consumption of substances prior to the event and trauma-related self-blame. Related studies had indicated a $d = 0.31$ to 0.5 and $\eta^2 = 0.43$ effect sizes between assault related substance consumption and self-blame (Blayney et al., 2016; Jaffe et al., 2018; Olszewski, 2009). An a priori analysis was conducted using G*power 3.1 software in order to determine an approximate sample size needed to power the analysis (Faul et al., 2009). With a power of 0.80 and a two-tailed alpha level of 0.05, the estimated sample size needed to obtain a 0.5 effect size was 128 participants, with at least 64 participants in each group, with groups separated by substance use or no substance use.

Based upon the range of sample sizes needed, the minimum number of participants needed for the purposes of this study is 200. This number was chosen in order to ensure sufficient power across all hypotheses. Only 179 participants could be obtained after data cleaning eliminated over 70 participants for incomplete or incorrect data. A post-hoc analysis was conducted using G*Power 3.1 software to assure sufficient power. The multiple regression analysis produced an effect size of $R^2 = 0.691$. Results of the post-hoc analysis indicated a power ($1-\beta$ err prob) of 1.00 with a critical t value of 1.97 indicating sufficient power to run the analysis.

Chapter III

Results

Data Management and Quality Control

The use of MTurk, a crowdsourcing marketplace, for psychological research has been an increasing trend over the past few years (Chmielewski & Kucker, 2019). Much of this recent research has shown that the quality of data collected through MTurk is equal or superior to data collected through other methods (Casler et al., 2013; Kees et al., 2017). In the last two or three years, some researchers have expressed more concerns with low quality data obtained through MTurk. Findings from one study indicated that low quality data can be mitigated by including validity indicators and screening MTurk data regularly (Chmielewski & Kucker, 2019). In order to assure high quality data collection through the online platform of MTurk for this study, various validity checks, data cleaning, and assumptions checks were utilized to assure high data quality. Validity checks are based on recommendations from Cheung and colleagues (2017).

First, the survey was designed in the Qualtrics platform using various logic and validity checks based on the inclusion/exclusion criteria and demographic questions which would remove participants from the study if they answered in the incorrect manner. By using the "Prevent Multiple Submissions" option on the Qualtrics platform, participants who attempted to re-enter the survey after being removed were unable to return (Qualtrics, 2022-a). The first four questions in the survey after the informed consent asked participants to answer "yes" or "no" to 1) I can speak and read English fluently, 2) I am a resident of the United States, 3) I have experienced a nonconsensual act at some point in my life (description included), 4) it has been at least four months since I experienced my last nonconsensual sexual event. If participants responded "no" to any of these questions they were sent to the end of the study after completing the fourth question and could not re-enter the survey with the same IP address. Additionally, a few of the demographic questions also acted as screeners that would remove participants from the study if answered incorrectly. If participants put their age as younger than 18, endorsed any gender identity other than cisgender man, and answered "no" to experiencing CSA and/or ASA they were also sent to the end of the study after completing the entire demographic section and unable to return with the same IP address. By allowing participants to answer multiple validity check questions before being removed from the study it significantly decreased the likelihood that participants would be able to determine which criteria eliminated them from the study, reset their cookies, and reenter the survey. Additionally, the recruitment flyer that was distributed through the MTurk platform did not provide details about the exact qualifications for participation in the study. By examining the inclusion/exclusion criteria and demographic questions, 51 respondents were eliminated for incorrectly answering one or more of these questions.

Although Qualtrics assures the same IP address will not be able to retake a survey either once the survey is completed or once they have been removed from the study, IP addresses were also double-checked to assure there were no duplicates. IP addresses were also checked to assure they resided within the U.S. The next two validity checks were part of the MTurk platform. Through this platform, MTurk workers are assigned a unique worker ID number when they register as a worker for the site. MTurk does not allow the same participant ID to complete multiple Human Intelligence Tasks (HIT)'s, which in survey language, indicates participants cannot complete multiple responses to the survey. Workers are only able to accept a HIT once and may only complete one HIT per assignment, thus significantly reducing the likelihood of repeated responders (Amazon Mechanical Turk, 2022-c). Workers are unable to create an additional worker profile unless they use a completely different name, email, and other identifying information. Secondly, when creating a HIT on MTurk there is the option to require Masters Workers, who are "workers that have consistently demonstrated a high degree of success in performing a wide range of HITs across a large number of Requesters" (Amazon Mechanical Turk, 2022-d). Masters Workers were used for this study.

The next validity check focused on time completion and patterned responses. The Qualtrics platform records the date/time participants begin and end the survey as well as how long, in seconds, it takes each participant to complete the entire survey. The estimated completion time for this survey per Qualtrics was 15 minutes, which is based on previous data that has found, the average human has a reading speed of 300 words/minute, it takes 500 milliseconds to transition between questions on a page, 300 milliseconds to transition between choices in a question, three seconds to transition between pages, two seconds to select slider question answers, and 10 seconds to type in a text-entry response (Qualtrics, 2022-b). For this survey, Qualtrics's time estimate included expected time it would take participants to read the entire text of the informed consent, debrief form, and multiple views of the resource list, which is unlikely, and thus 15 minutes may be an overestimate of the actual completion time. Descriptive statistics were run on the completion time data and findings indicated a mean of approximately 10 minutes with a standard deviation of approximately nine minutes (Table 1). Participants were excluded from the study if they took less than three minutes to complete the survey and there was a lack of variability in their survey responses. Participants who either provided flatlining responses, or routinely selected the same responses, or were seen to respond in a consistent pattern were removed. Overall, this procedure eliminated an additional 13 respondents from the study.

Table 1

Descriptive Statistics for Survey Time Completion in Seconds

Duration in Seconds	Minimum	Maximum	Mean	SD
2932.00	120.00	3052.00	659.58	593.61

Another level of validity checks involved reviewing patterns of consistency in participant responses to remove participants who displayed inconsistent responding across similar questions. On the MTurk platform, workers must be 18 years of age to complete HITs (Amazon Mechanical Turk, 2022-e). The Qualtrics survey also asked participants to provide their age with the option to provide an age under 18. Additionally, MTurk gives Requesters the option to add additional criteria, which will not allow workers who do not meet this criterion to be assigned to this specific HIT. For the purposes of this study, male gender was the added criteria. Then once participants started the Qualtrics survey they were asked to provide their gender and given options outside of cis-gender male. If participants provided any answer outside of cis-gender male, or an age lower than 18, they were removed from the study. Throughout the study, participants were asked on multiple occasions whether they had experienced CSA or ASA. In the inclusion criteria questions, participants were asked if they had experienced a nonconsensual sexual activity during their lifetime. If they answered "no," they were removed from the study. In the demographic section, participants were then asked two separate questions, one about CSA and one about ASA. If participants endorsed the inclusion criteria question correctly, but then endorsed both the CSA and ASA questions negatively, they were removed from the study.

Sample Characteristics

A total of 179 individuals participated in this survey and were utilized for the complete analysis of this study. A total of 252 individuals attempted to participate, though many were excluded for various reasons such as identifying as something other than cisgender male, not having experienced CSA or ASA, not being a U.S. resident, and/or too little time having passed since their last nonconsensual sexual event. A total of 51 participants were eliminated for these reasons. Another 17 participants were eliminated due to validity concerns including failing out of the study due to a lack of completion within the required time frame, having too much missing data, completing the survey too quickly, and/or responding in a consistent or patterned manner. All participants utilized in the analyses identified themselves as cisgender male SV survivors, living within the U.S., fluent in English, and at least 18 years of age.

General Demographic Composition

Participants ranged from 23 to 91 years old (Figure 4), with a mode of 30 years and a median age of 31 years (*SD* = 10.65). As shown in Table 2, the sample was predominantly White (83.8%), with the remainder of the sample including American Indian/Alaskan Native (6.7%), Asian/Asian American/Pacific Islander (5%), Black/African American (2.8%), Biracial (1.1%), and Other (0.6%). While the survey was designed to allow participants to indicate multiple ethnic identities, no one selected more than one or provided additional information when they identified as biracial, thus, no more detail was obtained for participants who selected this identity. This sample was largely White (Figure 4) and non-Hispanic (Figure 3), which represents only some of the individuals who are impacted by ASA and CSA. In terms of sexual orientation, 58.1% reported identifying as heterosexual, 34.1% Bisexual, 6.1% Asexual, and 1.7% Gay (Figure 2). Other sexual orientation options were provided including Queer, Pansexual, Other, and Prefer Not to Say, however, no participants selected these options. Compared to the overall national statistics, this sample was slightly more diverse when compared to sexual orientation representation for men. In the United States currently 90.1% of men identify as heterosexual, 2.0% bisexual, 2.5% gay, and 0.2% as something else (Jones, 2022).

Over three fourths of the sample (76.5%) reported having experienced CSA ($n = 137$), 86.6% reported having experienced ASA ($n = 155$), and 70.4% reported having experienced both CSA and ASA ($n = 126$). This compares to data from the total population of the United States: out of the total number of men who have experienced SV, 48.7% men first experienced it in adulthood and 51.3% reported having their first experience before the age of 18 (CDC, 2018).

Figure 1

Sample Distribution: Age

Table 2

Frequencies and Percentages for Categorical Variables

Variable	*N*	%
Race		
White/Caucasian	150	83.8
American Indian/Alaskan Native	12	6.7
Asian/Asian American/Pacific Is.	9	5.0
Black/African American	5	2.8
Biracial	2	1.1
Other	1	0.6
Ethnicity		
Hispanic or Latino	38	21.2
Non-Hispanic or Latino	141	78.8
Sexual Orientation		
Heterosexual	104	58.1
Bisexual	61	34.1
Asexual	11	6.1
Gay	3	1.7
Nonconsensual Sexual Event		
Childhood Sexual Abuse (CSA)	24	13.4
Adult Sexual Assault (ASA)	29	16.2
Both CSA & ASA	126	70.4

Descriptive Statistics

The means and standard deviations of all study variables can be seen in Table 3.

Per self-report in the demographics, 72.6% ($n = 130$) of participants reported consuming alcohol or other substances prior to their CSA and/or ASA event (Figure 5). This is approximately the same as statistics reported for the general population, with studies indicating approximately 70% of men used substances before their nonconsensual sexual event (Reed et al., 2009; Relyea & Ullman, 2015).

In exploratory analyses of relationships between self-blame and demographic factors and scores on various test measures. Findings indicate age was significantly negatively correlated with self-blame ($r = -.295$; $p = <.001$) and significantly positively correlated with total unsupportive disclosure responses ($r = .464$; $p = .01$), physiological arousal ($r = .524$; $p = <.001$) TI symptoms ($r = .343$; $p = <.001$), rape myth acceptance ($r = .658$; $p = <.001$), total ASA experiences ($r = .278$; $p = <.001$), and total combined CSA and ASA experiences ($r = .183$; $p = .14$) and substance use prior to their nonconsensual sexual events ($r = .241$; $p = .01$).

The Sexual Experiences Survey – Short Form - Victimization (SES-SFV) was used to calculate the number of experiences participants had survived out of the five different categories described. Sexual acts experienced only in childhood or CSA ($M = 1.06$, $SD = 1.51$), only in adulthood or ASA ($M = 1.66$, $SD = 1.5$), and events experienced both in childhood and adulthood ($M = 1.25$, $SD = 1.50$). A small percentage of participants (24; 13.6%) reported at least one sexual abuse experience only during childhood. Likewise, (29; 16.2%) reported at least one sexual assault experience only during adulthood, and 126 (70.4%) reported having experienced both CSA and ASA (Figure 9). Overall, 51.4% ($n = 92$) reported experiencing more than one CSA or ASA event in their lifetime and 31.3% (56) reported having experienced more than one nonconsensual sexual event within the last 12 months. Due to IRB requiring SES-SFV questions to be adjusted to remove the questions regarding how many total times an individual experienced each nonconsensual sexual event, the total number of events across the entire lifetime could not be calculated.

The Checklist of Sexual Abuse and Related Stressors (CSARS) was utilized to measure disclosures and unsupportive disclosure responses. Approximately 64.2% ($n = 115$) of participants stated that they had never disclosed their nonconsensual sexual event(s; Figure 6), which is slightly lower than the 74% seen in national statistics (RAINN, 2019). Of the 64 participants who did disclose, 92% ($n = 59$) reported they received at least one unsupportive disclosure response. The range of scores on this measure were from 0 to 7, with most participants scoring between a 2 and 4 ($M = 3.08$, $SD = 1.33$). Characterological self-blame was significantly positively correlated with participants negative disclosure experiences ($r = .464$; $p = <.001$).

The Gender-Inclusive Illinois Rape Myth Acceptance Scale (GIIRMA) was utilized to measure participants beliefs in common rape myths. A large portion of participants (136; 76%) reported significant beliefs in rape myths. Regarding the added rape myth question of "men cannot be raped," 68 (38%) participants stated they either Agree or Strongly Agree with this statement and 55 (31%) Strongly Disagreed with this statement. Two participants (1%) reported the maximum score on the measure ($M = 60.86$, $SD = 18.68$). Exact rates of RMA in the general population have not been obtained, but various studies generally indicate a large percentage of both men and women endorse believing at least one rape myth (Walfield, 2018).

The Tonic Immobility Scale (TIS) measured the number of TI symptoms experienced during their most recent ASA or CSA experience. Almost all ($n = 171$; 95%) participants reported having experienced significant TI and ($n = 164$; 91%) participants reported experiencing significant fear during their most recent sexual assault. A total of nine participants (5%) reported the maximum score on the measure ($M = 51.25$, $SD = 10.84$). This is higher than in past studies, which have reported between 58-63% (Hodge & Canter, 1998). The range of scores on this measure were from 1 to 60.

The Subjective Physiological Sexual Arousal Rating Scale measured the intensity of physiological arousal sensations during their most recent nonconsensual sexual event. Only five (2.8%) participants indicated experiencing no indications of physiological arousal. Over half of the participants reported significant experiences of physiological arousal ($n = 108$; 60%). This number is higher than the 20% previous studies have previously reported (Bullock & Beckson, 2011). Lastly, eight participants (4.5%) reported the maximum score on the measure ($M = 34.63$, $SD = 10.02$).

The Rape Attribution Questionnaire (RAQ) measured the levels of self-blame related to participants' CSA and/or ASA traumatic experiences. Only 7.3%, ($n = 13$) reported not endorsing any self-blame, with 8.9% ($n = 16$) reporting no characterological self-blame ($M = 14.11$, $SD = 4.63$) and 9.5% (17) reporting no behavioral self-blame ($M = 14.42$, $SD = 4.57$). The range of scores on this measure were from 10 to 50 ($M = 28.53$, $SD = 8.73$).

Table 3

Descriptive Statistics of Study Variables

Measure	Mean	*SD*	Range
GIIRMA	60.31	18.79	76.00
TIS	51.25	10.84	48.00
Arousal	34.63	10.02	42.00
CSARS	3.08	1.33	5.00
SES-SFV	1.25	1.49	5.00
RAQ	28.53	8.73	40.00

Note. GIIRMA = Gender-Inclusive Illinois Rape Myth Acceptance Scale; TIS = Tonic Immobility Scale; Arousal = Subjective Physiological Sexual Arousal Rating Scale; CSARS = Sexual Abuse and Related Stressors; SES-SFV = Sexual Experiences Survey – Short Form – Victimization; RAQ = Rape Attribution Scale

Figure 5

Sample Distribution: Consumption of Substances

Hypothesis Tests

Assumptions

A multiple regression was conducted to assess Hypothesis 1, Hypothesis 2, Hypothesis 3, Hypothesis 4b, and Hypothesis 6 with self-blame as the dependent variable and number of nonconsensual sexual events in both childhood/adulthood, rape myth acceptance (RMA), TI, unsupportive disclosure responses, and physiological sexual arousal as predictor variables, respectively.

Tests to see if the data met the assumption of linearity were not violated as all correlations between the predictors and outcome variable were non-zero (Nonconsensual Events $r = .21$ RMA & Self-blame $r = .67$; TI & Self-blame $r = .11$; Disclosure & Self-blame $r = .46$; Arousal & Self-blame $r = .43$). Tests to see if the data met the assumption of collinearity indicated that multicollinearity was not a concern (Nonconsensual Events, Tolerance = .927, VIF = 1.078; RMA, Tolerance = .679, VIF = 1.472; Disclosure, Tolerance = .504, VIF = 1.98; Tonic Immobility, Tolerance = .587, VIF = 1.703; Arousal, Tolerance = .380, VIF = 2.630). The data also met the assumption of independent errors (Durbin-Watson value = 1.847). The histogram of standardized residuals (Figure 11) indicated that the data contained approximately normally distributed errors for self-blame, as did the normal P-P plot of standardized residuals, which showed points that were not completely on the line, but close (Figure 10). Unfortunately, according to the Mahalanobis' critical distance calculator there were two multivariate outliers (23.89 & 20.39) with a critical value greater than 18.902. These are considered minor outliers and were left in the dataset due to the fact they are not large enough to significantly change the outcome of the data. Lastly, according to the Loess line, data did not violate the assumption of homoscedasticity (Figure 12).

A Kolmogorov-Smirnov test indicated that self-blame, nonconsensual sexual events, RMA, unsupportive disclosure responses and arousal followed a normal distribution. Skewness and Kurtosis were examined to determine how much the data differed from a normal distribution. An analysis of Z-scores was carried out and revealed that the majority of variables did not have any outliers and all data fit within the parameters of -3 and +3 (Nonconsensual Sexual Events = -8.39 to 2.51; RMA = -2.76 to 1.82; Disclosure = -0.84 to 2.51; Arousal = -2.76 to 1.43; Self-Blame = -2.12 to 2.46). The TI measure, the TIS, had two outliers at 3.36 and 3.00 these two scores were transformed using the Winsorize method and substituted for the next highest value that is not an outlier (Erceg-Hurn & Mirosevich, 2008). The scores for the two outliers were 14 and 18 and the next highest value that was not an outlier was 22, so both scores were adjusted to 22, which eliminated any outliers (TIS = -2.70 to 1.73). This signifies that the data was not symmetrical but not too extreme to require a non-parametric test (Ernst & Albers, 2017). Additionally, a multiple regression is considered a robust test with respect to violations of the assumption of normality (Ernst & Albers, 2017). Thus, the current results can still be considered reliable and valid. The scatterplot of standardized residuals showed that the data met the assumptions of homogeneity of variance and linearity. The data also met the assumption of non-zero variances.

A t-test was conducted to assess Hypothesis 4a. Both samples were independent and obtained using a random sampling method. A test of normality was conducted by visually checking a normal Q-Q plot of standardized residuals which showed points that were relatively close to the line. Levene's test indicated equal variances, F (2, 177) = 1.32, p = .252.

A t-test was conducted to assess Hypothesis 5. Both samples were independent and obtained using a random sampling method. A normal Q-Q plot of standardized residuals revealed a violation of the assumption of normality. Levene's test indicated unequal variances, F (2, 177) = .971, p = .326. The t-test is considered a robust statistical analysis and thus the results can still be considered valid and reliable (Keselman et al., 2003).

Figure 10

P-P Plot of Standardized Residuals for Self-Blame

Total Prediction Model

A multiple regression was used to determine if any of the predictor variables (number of nonconsensual sexual event categories experiences in both childhood/adulthood, rape myth acceptance, TI, unsupportive disclosure responses, and sexual arousal) would significantly predict self-blame. Results indicated that this was a significant prediction model, F (5, 58) = 10.602, $p < .001$ (Table 6), with a large effect size $R^2 = 0.69$ (Table 4), suggesting that 47.8% of the variance in self-blame can be accounted for by the five predictors, collectively. The predicted self-blame is equal to 10.602 + 0.371 (sexual event categories) + 0.260 (rape myth acceptance) - .134 (TI) + 0.914 (unsupportive disclosure) + 0.097 (sexual arousal), per one unit increase in each factor. Looking at the individual contributions of the predictors, the results show that only rape myth acceptance ($\beta = 0.557$, $t = 4.315$, $p < .001$) was significant. This suggests that male survivors who endorse stronger beliefs in various rape myths endorse higher levels of trauma-related self-blame. An additional analysis was run adding in age as predictor variable. Results indicated this was a significant predictor model F (6, 57) = 9.958, $p < .001$ (Table 6), with a very large effect size $R^2 = 0.72$ (Table 4), suggesting that 51.2% of the variance in self-blame can be accounted for by age by the five predictors. Age was a significant predictor ($\beta = -.230$, $t = -1.999$, $p = .05$). This suggests that as male survivors age they endorse lower levels of trauma-related self-blame.

A multiple regression analysis was also used to determine if any of the predictor variables mentioned above would significantly predict only characterological self-blame. Results indicated that this was also a significant prediction model, F (5, 58) = 9.901, $p < .001$, with a very large effect size $R^2 = 0.68$, suggesting that 46% of the variance in characterological self-blame can be accounted for by the five predictors, collectively. The predicted self-blame is equal to 10.602 +

0.286 (sexual event categories) + 0.118 (rape myth acceptance) - 0.076 (TI) + 0.669 (unsupportive disclosure) + 0.060 (sexual arousal), per one unit increase in each factor. Looking at the individual contributions of the predictors, the results show that only rape myth acceptance ($\beta = 0.479$, $t = 3.689$, $p = <.001$) was significant. This suggests that male survivors who endorse stronger beliefs in various rape myths endorse higher levels of trauma-related characterological self-blame.

A multiple regression analysis was also used to determine if any of the predictor variables mentioned above would significantly predict only behavioral self-blame. Results indicated that this was also a significant prediction model, F (5, 58) = 8.489, $p < .001$, with a large effect size $R^2 = 0.650$, suggesting that 42.3% of the variance in characterological self-blame can be accounted for by the five predictors, collectively. The predicted self-blame is equal to 10.602 + 0.085 (sexual event categories) + 0.142 (rape myth acceptance) - 0.058 (TI) + 0.245 (unsupportive disclosure) + 0.038 (sexual arousal), per one unit increase in each factor. Looking at the individual contributions of the predictors, the results show that again, only rape myth acceptance ($\beta = 0.577$, $t = 4.295$, $p <.001$) was significant. This suggests that male survivors who endorse stronger beliefs in various rape myths endorse higher levels of trauma-related behavioral self-blame.

A multiple regression analysis was also used to determine if sexual event categories experienced in both childhood and adulthood, only in childhood, and only in adulthood would significantly predict self-blame. Results indicated that this was a significant prediction model, F (3, 175) = 10.595, $p < .001$ (Table 7), with a small effect size $R^2 = 0.15$ (Table 7), suggesting that 15.4% of the variance in self-blame can be accounted for the three predictors, collectively. The predicted self-blame is equal to 10.595 + 0.292 (both in childhood and adulthood) + 0.386 (only in adulthood) + 0.160 (only in childhood), per one unit increase in each factor. Looking at the individual contributions of the predictors, the results show that the both in childhood and adulthood ($\beta = 0.292$, $t = 3.091$, $p <.001$) and only in adulthood categories ($\beta = 0.386$, $t = 4.914$, $p <.001$) were significant. This suggests that male survivors who experienced a higher number of sexual events in both childhood and adulthood and only in adulthood endorse higher levels of trauma-related self-blame.

Hypothesis 1

Hypothesis 1 predicted that the number of nonconsensual sexual event categories experienced in both childhood and adulthood would significantly and positively predict self-blame. The hypothesis was not supported by the results, as indicated by a non-significant positive relationship between SES-SFV category scores and RAQ scores (Figure 13). Nonconsensual sexual event categories endorsed in childhood and adulthood did not contribute to the multiple regression model ($\beta = .063$, $p = 0.527$; Table 6).

A separate *t*-test analysis was also run for this hypothesis to determine if individuals who experienced various nonconsensual sexual event categories in both childhood and adulthood endorsed higher levels of self-blame than individuals who endorsed having these experiences in only childhood or adulthood. Results indicated that self-blame was significantly greater for those who endorsed experiences in both childhood and adulthood ($M = 30.93$, $SD = 6.46$) than for those who endorsed in either childhood or adulthood ($M = 25.69$, $SD = 10.10$); $t\,(177) = 4.23$, $p <.001$. The hypothesis was supported by the results, indicated a significant difference in self-blame between those who experienced various sexual events in childhood and adulthood versus those who only experienced these events in either childhood or adulthood (Figure 14).

Figure 13

Scatterplot of Number of Nonconsensual Sexual Event Categories and Self-Blame

Note. RAQ Total = Total score on measure of self-blame, Rape Attribution Questionnaire; SES_SFV Total = Total score on categories of nonconsensual sexual events experienced in both childhood and adulthood, Sexual Experiences Survey – Short Form – Victimization

Figure 14

Bar Sexual Events Both CSA & ASA vs. Either CSA or ASA and Average Self-Blame

Note. RAQ Total = Total score on measure of self-blame, Rape Attribution Questionnaire; SES_SFV Both vs. Either = Nonconsensual sexual event categories where 0 indicates an event experienced only in childhood or adulthood and 1 indicates an event experienced in both childhood and adulthood, Sexual Experiences Survey – Short Form – Victimization

Hypothesis 2

It was hypothesized rape myth acceptance would significantly and positively predict self-blame. A multiple regression was utilized (Table 4). The hypothesis was supported by the results, as indicated by a significant relationship between GIIRMA and RAQ scores (Figure 15). Rape myth acceptance significantly contributed to the multiple regression model (β = .551, p <.001; Table 6).

Figure 15

Scatterplot of Rape Myth Acceptance and Self-Blame

Note. RAQ Total = Total score on measure of self-blame, Rape Attribution Questionnaire; GIIRMA Total = Total score on measure of rape myth acceptance, Gender-Inclusive Illinois Rape Myth Acceptance Scale.

Hypothesis 3

It was hypothesized that TI would significantly and positively predict self-blame. A multiple regression was utilized (Table 4). The hypothesis was not supported by the results, as indicated by a non-significant, negative relationship between TIS and RAQ scores (Figure 16). Tonic immobility did not contribute to the multiple regression model ($\beta = -.155, p = 0.216$; Table 6).

Figure 16

Scatterplot of Tonic Immobility and Self-Blame

Note. RAQ Total = Total score on measure of self-blame, Rape Attribution Questionnaire; TIS = Total score on the measure of TI, Tonic Immobility Scale.

Hypothesis 4a

It was hypothesized that levels of self-blame would be higher for those who have never disclosed their CSA or ASA than for those who have disclosed. An independent samples *t-test* was conducted to determine whether there was a significant between groups difference of self-blame between those who had disclosed and those who had not. Results indicated that self-blame was significantly greater for those who did not disclose ($M = 39.12$, $SD = 8.26$) than for those who did disclose ($M = 25.66$, $SD = 8.88$); $t\,(177) = -3.75$, $p < .001$. The hypothesis was supported by the results, indicating a significant difference in self-blame between those who disclosed their SV and those who did not (Figure 19). It is important to note, directionality of the relationship between self-blame and disclosure cannot be determined due to the correlational nature of this analysis.

Figure 17

Bar Graph of Unsupportive Disclosure Responses and Average Self-Blame

Note. Disclosed to Someone = Disclosure screener question where 0 indicates no disclosure and 1 indicates disclosure to a friend or family member; Mean RAQ Total = Average total score on measure of self-blame, Rape Attribution Questionnaire.

Hypothesis 4b

It was hypothesized that unsupportive disclosure responses would significantly and positively predict self-blame. A multiple regression was utilized (Table 4). The hypothesis was not supported by the results; there was no significant relationship between unsupportive disclosure responses and self-blame (Figure 17). Unsupportive disclosure responses did not contribute to the multiple regression model ($\beta = .136, p = 0.315$; *Table 6).*

Figure 18

Scatterplot of Unsupportive Disclosure Responses and Self-Blame

Note. RAQ Total = Total score on measure of self-blame, Rape Attribution Questionnaire; CSARS Total = Total score on measure of unsupportive disclosure responses, Checklist of Sexual Abuse and Related Stressors

Hypothesis 5

It was hypothesized that levels of self-blame would be higher for those who consumed substances prior to their CSA or ASA than for those who did not consume substances. An independent samples *t*-test was conducted to determine whether there was a significant between groups difference of self-blame between those who had consumed substances and those who had not. Results indicated that self-blame was significantly greater for those who did consume substances ($M = 29.82$, $SD = 8.35$) than for those who did consume substances ($M = 25.10$, $SD = 8.86$); $t\ (177) = 3.311$, $p = .001$. The hypothesis was supported by the results, indicating a significant difference in self-blame between those who consumed substances prior to their sexual trauma and those who did not (Figure 20).

Figure 19

Bar Graph of Substances Consumed and Average Self-Blame

Note. Substances Used = Screener question related to substance use prior to sexual assault where 0 indicates no consumption of substances and 1 indicates consumption of substances prior to the sexual trauma; Mean RAQ Total = Average total score on measure of self-blame, Rape Attribution Questionnaire.

Hypothesis 6

It was hypothesized that physiological sexual arousal would significantly and positively predict self-blame. A multiple regression was utilized (Table 4). The hypothesis was not supported by the results, as indicated by a non-significant, positive relationship between Arousal and RAQ scores (Figure 18). Physiological sexual arousal did not contribute to the multiple regression model ($\beta = .111, p = 0.476$; Table 6).

Figure 20

Scatterplot of Physiological Sexual Arousal and Self-Blame

Note. RAQ Total = Total score on measure of self-blame, Rape Attribution Questionnaire; Arousal Total = Total score on measure of physiological sexual arousal, Subjective Physiological Sexual Arousal Rating Scale.

Table 4

Model Summary: Self-Blame

Model	R	R^2	Adjusted R^2	Std. Error	R^2 Change	F Change	df1	df2	Sig F Change	Durbin-Watson
1	.650	.423	.373	3.668	.423	8.489	5	58	<.001	2.242

Table 5

One Way Analysis of Variances for Multiple Regression of Self-Blame

Model	Sum of Squares	*Df*	Mean Square	*F*	sig
Regression	571.211	5	114.242	8.489	<.001
Residual	780.524	58	13.457		
Total	1351.734	63			

Note. Dependent Variable: Self-blame as measured by Rape Attribution Questionnaire (RAQ). Predictors: Rape Myth Acceptance (GIIRMA), Tonic Immobility (TIS), Physiological Sexual Arousal (Arousal), Unsupportive Disclosure Responses (CSARS), and Nonconsensual Sexual Event Categories (SES-SFV).

Table 6

Coefficient Regression: Self-Blame

	Unstandardized Coefficients		Standardized Coefficients			95% Confidence Interval		Collinearity Statistics	
Model	Beta	Std. Error	Beta	*t*	Sig.	Lower Bound	Upper Bound	Tolerance	VIF
(Constant)	10.39	4.85		2.14	0.37	.674	20.11		
GIIRMA	.142	.033	.577	4.30	<.001	.140	.381	.552	1.81
TIS	-.134	.107	-.155	1.25	.216	-.350	.081	.586	1.71
Arousal	.097	.136	.111	.717	.476	-.175	.369	.379	2.64
CSARS	.914	.901	.136	1.01	.315	-.890	2.72	.498	2.01
SES-SFV	.371	.583	.063	.636	.527	.796	1.54	.927	1.08

Note. GIIRMA = Gender-Inclusive Illinois Rape Myth Acceptance Scale; TIS = Tonic Immobility Scale, Arousal = Subjective Physiological Sexual Arousal Rating Scale; CSARS =

Checklist of Sexual Abuse and Related Stressors; SES-SFV = Sexual Experiences Survey – Short Form – Victimization

Table 7

Model Summary: Self-Blame and Sexual Event Categories

Model	*R*	R^2	Adjusted R^2	Std. Error	R^2 Change	*F* Change	df1	df2	Sig *F* Change	Durbin-Watson
1	.392	.154	.139	8.097	.154	10.595	3	175	<.001	1.654

Chapter IV

Discussion

The aims of this study were to examine the relationship between characteristics of nonconsensual sexual experiences and the trauma-related self-blame internalized by male survivors. Specifically, it aimed to explore whether cisgender men who experienced ASA and/or CSA that involved TI, unsupportive disclosure responses, physiological sexual arousal, and/or consumption of substances, and ascribe to various rape myths, endorse greater self-blame associated with the event compared to individuals who did not have these experiences. The present study examined the self-report experiences of 179 cisgender male survivors of sexual traumas gathered by means of a MTurk nationwide online survey. A deeper understanding of unique characteristics of survivor's experiences will help to inform future treatment models and interventions with this population.

Compared to the U.S. population, the sample obtained in this study was less racially diverse. About 84% of the sample identified as White, whereas U.S. Census data suggests only about 61% of males in the U.S. are White (Jones et al., 2021). This disparity between the sample demographic and racial percentages in the population call into question the generalizability of this research to the larger population. Due to American Indian/Alaskan Native, Asian/Asian America, Black, and Biracial individuals being underrepresented in this study, there are concerns the findings from this study may not accurately describe these groups' unique experiences. This lack of representation of minority communities is especially concerning due to the increased prevalence rates of SV among these groups. Native Americans are at the highest risk for ASA and are two times more likely to experience ASA than any other racial group, with 56.1% of women and 27.5% of men experiencing some form of SV (NSVRC, 2019; RAINN, 2017).

Although racial demographics are more difficult to determine for male survivors of SV, some research has shown that 3.3% of Black men 4.4% of Biracial men will experience at least one nonconsensual sexual event in their lifetime, compared to 2% of White men (RAINN, 2017). Even though the rates are likely higher than what current statistics indicate within these communities, these survivors are much less likely to disclose their abuse. Previous research has shown that Black individuals are significantly less likely to disclose their experiences of abuse due to historical experiences of marginalization, rejection, and systemic oppression (Slatton & Richard, 2020). The sample for this study was likely heavily White due to minority communities' fears of sharing their experiences because of previous negative experiences, cultural insensitivity, and/or lack of support from systems of care. For future research, it would be beneficial to directly target these minority communities to obtain information on their unique experiences to provide individualized support and treatment to meet their needs. It is imperative that research on self-blame experiences for racial minority survivors of SV be captured to identify similarities and differences between the dominant cultural group to tailor therapeutic approaches as needed.

Regarding sexual orientation diversity in the study, the sample was significantly more diverse when compared to U.S. Census data. Only 58% of the sample identified as heterosexual, whereas U.S. Census data suggests over 90% of cisgender males identify as heterosexual. Additionally, U.S. Census data indicates only 2.5% of cisgender males identify as bisexual and 4.3% identify as gay (File et al., 2021). Sample characteristics from this study were very different, with over 30% of participants identifying as bisexual and only 1.7% identifying as gay, with the additional 6.1% identifying as asexual. There are a few possible reasons for these discrepancies. It is important to note that a smaller portion of the general male population have experienced ASA or CSA; likely some between 3-31%, compared to females. Whereas other research has shown SV rates are significantly higher for both sexual and gender minority groups (Beyer et al., 2020; NSVRC, 2019). Potentially, the sample characteristics for this study are more accurately representative of the sub-group of men who are more likely to experience SV, which is skewed towards sexual and gender minority groups.

Another potential reason for the lower number of heterosexual cisgender men who completed this study, when compared to the U.S. Census data, is related to continued stigmatization and gender bias. In general, men are much less likely to disclose their experiences of sexual abuse than women. This is often due to beliefs surrounding masculinity norms, rape myths about men being unable to be sexually assaulted, and homophobic beliefs (Pratt, 2022; Smith, 2020). It is possible these factors influenced heterosexual men's willingness to participate in this survey due to internalized beliefs and/or unacknowledged rape (Reed et al., 2020).

This study was unable to provide significant detailed evidence that self-blame experiences differ based on both/either racial, ethnic, or sexual orientation identities due to the small number of participants in many of these groups. Although inferences could not be made about every unique group, there was enough information to show that racial identities such as Asian/Asian American/Pacific Islander and White/Caucasian were significantly predictive of self-blame whereas the identity Black/African American was not predictive of self-blame. The Asian/Asian American/Pacific Islander identity was also the only identity that was significantly predictive of TI experiences. Also, the American Indian/Alaskan Native identity did not significantly predict self-blame, arousal, TI, or rape myth acceptance. Additionally, Bisexual identities were significantly predictive of self-blame and rape myth acceptance, whereas Heterosexual identities were predictive of significant arousal experiences, and rape myth acceptance. Asexual identities were not predictive of any of the identified factors and there were not enough individuals who identified as Gay and Biracial to run separate analyses on.

These data trends suggest there are vastly different experiences not only of self-blame but also experiences directly related to the nonconsensual sexual events. Sexual orientation and racial identities may significantly impact survivors' perceptions of their experiences of SV while also impacting how they internalize these experiences. One explanation of these findings is there are unique cultural factors within groups that may either protect them from the more negative outcomes of SV or may prime them to have more substantial negative outcomes. Another explanation is there were just not large enough samples of these various groups to accurately describe the experiences of the larger populations. Future research should stive to explore more in-depth how various demographic factors may either protect from or predict stronger self-blame experiences to be able to identify and treat these symptoms more effectively.

Hypothesis 1 predicted that the number of nonconsensual sexual event categories in childhood and/or adulthood, as measured by the Sexual Experiences Survey – Short Form – Victimization (SES-SFV), would be predictive of self-blame, as measured by the Rape Attribution Questionnaire (RAQ); this prediction was not supported, although there was still a statistically significant correlation. The correlation between frequency of sexual events and self-blame is important since much of the previous research has shown more significant symptomatology and higher rates of self-blame for individuals who have experienced more than one nonconsensual sexual event (Pratt, 2022; Zink et al., 2009). Additionally, increased rates of self-blame have been seen to lead to worse adaptive coping, increased PTSD symptoms, and increased likelihood of revictimization (Brietenbecher, 2006; Ullman et al., 2014). One hypothesis for why results from this study did not support the previous research findings is due to the adjustments that IRB required be made to the SES-SFV measure, which only allowed for participants to answer "yes/no" for if they experienced a certain event. The adjustments IRB required did not allow participants to indicate whether all sexual acts had occurred during one singular event, or multiple times during separate events across the lifetime. Thus, individuals who were identified as having more "yes" responses to this survey, may not have necessarily experienced a higher frequency of events.

Although a higher number of nonconsensual sexual event categories was not predictive of self-blame in this study, there was a correlation between these two variables. This indicates that although revictimization may not predict the level of severity of trauma-related self-blame, there is still a relationship between the two variables. This finding is supported in previous literature, with multiple researchers finding a bi-directional relationship between self-blame and revictimization (Bernstein et al., 2022; Breitenbecher, 2006; Miller et al., 2007). The strength of the correlation between revictimization and self-blame is important to consider since past research has also shown both factors are predictive of lower rates of self-disclosure and help seeking behaviors (Sigurvinsdottir et al., 2019; Ullman et al., 2014). For individuals who end up stuck in the cycle of self-blame and revictimization, there is an even further increased likelihood they will experience severe and long-term psychological impacts. It is also important to consider how self-blame and psychological functioning may be impacted for men who receive mental health treatment for an initial nonconsensual sexual event but then continue to be sexually victimized. This is also an important consideration for children who are victims of CSA, receive treatment in childhood, but then end up revictimized in adulthood.

Hypothesis 2 predicted that higher levels of rape myth acceptance (RMA) as measured by the Gender-Inclusive Illinois Rape Myth Acceptance Scale (GIIRMA), would be predictive of self-blame, as measured by the Rape Attribution Questionnaire (RAQ). This prediction was supported in the present study and RMA was also found to be a significantly positively correlated with self-blame. These findings are supported by past research which has shown a strong relationship between RMA, unacknowledged rape, and self-blame, which are all correlated with lower disclosure rates, which often lead to worse psychological outcomes (Reed et al., 2020). When survivors already hold strong accepting beliefs regarding general rape myths, these are likely to be only further reinforced by their own experiences of SV (Lutz-Zois et al., 2015). Additionally, continued lack of disclosure and discussion of common rape myths continues to perpetuate the stigma often surrounding SV, especially for men. This just continues the cycle of men being less likely to disclose, leading them to not receive the treatment that could support them in restructuring their beliefs, leading people to further avoid de-stigmatizing rape within the larger community.

For this study specifically, the rape myth "men cannot be raped" was added to the GIIRMA assessment measure to determine if endorsement in this belief alone was predictive of self-blame. The prediction was supported by the results indicating the detrimental nature of this rape myth on its own. This finding is especially concerning due to the higher rate of men who often endorse believing rape myths which is frequently tied to sexism, gender stereotypes, and heteronormative beliefs (Walfield, 2020). Acceptance in this rape myth has also been tied to the belief that men who do have the courage to disclose or report their nonconsensual sexual events are making false reports, leading to further stigmatization and rejection which likely further increases self-blame (Walfield, 2020). These findings support the need for increased discussions and psychoeducation about rape myths with the larger population as a means of early intervention. These conversations should be happening as early possible to prevent young boys from latching on to inaccurate, stigmatizing, and sexist beliefs after experiencing CSA.

Hypothesis 3 predicted that higher levels of TI during the assault, as measured by the Tonic Immobility Scale (TIS), would be predictive of self-blame, as measured by the Rape Attribution Questionnaire (RAQ). This prediction was not supported in the present study. Although TI was not seen to predict self-blame, there was still a medium correlation between the two, indicating some type of interaction and relationship. TI is an involuntary response that is believed to be a basic survival instinct and connected to the fight-flight response (Gallup & Rager, 1996). It involves a complete physical immobility while the victim remains cognitively aware of what is happening without the ability to defend themselves, which is elicited by extreme fear (Bovin et al., 2014). It is a common misconception among survivors of SV, that they are somehow at fault for not fighting back during the sexual act, when in reality, they have no control over this response.

There are a few potential reasons why the TI findings from this study may have deviated from findings in other studies. One potential reason for the current findings is these results are a true representation of the male experience. For men, TI experiences may not consistently predict self-blame, although these two factors may still be correlated. Part of these findings could be since so much of the previous research on TI during sexual assault and the connection to self-blame has been conducted on women, meaning there is very little data exploring this relationship with men (Coxell & King, 2010). Much of the early research on TI found that physical restraint was needed to elicit a TI response, but more recent research has found that a belief in the lack of ability to escape is enough (Gallup, 1977; Gallup & Rager, 1996). Potentially, for men, true physical restraint is needed in order for a strong TI response to emerge. It is possible that full TI responses may be less common in men, or experienced differently, which may not have been picked up on in the TIS. The TIS was also developed through use primarily with a female population, which is another important consideration in this study's results. The TIS was also developed as a two-factor measure, picking up on both immobility experiences and fear responses, so it is possible men may experience one of these factors more strongly than women or vice versa.

Most of the previous research has found a strong connection between TI responses and self-blame, guilt, and shame, which is then related to various negative outcomes such as slower recovery from symptoms, and increased depression and anxiety (Hagenaars & Hagenaars, 2020). Some research has also found that although TI experiences may predict negative beliefs about others and the world, they did not predict negative self-beliefs (Buren & Weierich, 2015). It is also possible that since TI is such a misunderstood phenomenon that is not regularly talked about, participants in this survey were confused or disconcerted by questions being asked or could not remember the specifics of their own bodily reactions during the nonconsensual sexual event.

Even though the TI findings from this study do not exactly align with previous research, it is still important to consider what these findings mean and how they may impact survivors. Much of the previous research assessed experiences of female survivors, used qualitative data, collected from college campuses, and only assessed individuals who were willing to disclose and seek out treatment (Buren & Weierich, 2015; Heidt et al., 2005; Moller et al., 2017; Pratt, 2022). Whereas, this research examined experiences of male survivors, most of whom had never disclosed or sought treatment, and had age and sexual orientation diversity. This specific research survey also did not ask about symptoms of PTSD, nor did it screen for other specific mental health symptoms. Previous studies have found strong correlation between TI and PTSD symptoms, slower recovery, and increased depression and anxiety (Buren & Weierich, 2015; Hagenaars & Hagenaars, 2020; Heidt et al., 2005). Further research should evaluate whether TI may be predictive of different mental health outcomes for male survivors compared to their female counterparts.

Hypothesis 4a predicted that survivors who had disclosed their nonconsensual sexual event, as measured by a screener in the demographic questions, would have significantly lower self-blame, as measured by the Rape Attribution Questionnaire (RAQ), than individuals who had not disclosed. Thus, individuals who do not disclose would experience more trauma-related self-blame. This prediction was supported in the present study. These findings are consistent with some of the literature. A few studies found improved psychological outcomes, reduced development of PTSD symptomatology, improved psychological well-being, and decreased self-blame after disclosure (Broman-Fulks et al., 2007; Jacques-Tiura et al., 2010; Milliken et al., 2016). But some of the past research has also found negative outcomes after disclosure. Some research has found that early disclosure may lead to an exacerbation of mental health symptoms, implying worse self-blame, or be completely unrelated to any mental health outcomes (O'Leary et al., 2010; Ullman & Filipas, 2005). One important factor to consider is that delayed disclosure likely makes it more challenging for survivors to receive therapeutic interventions and appropriate support, which could lead to negative psychopathology, increased shame, guilt, and stronger beliefs in their responsibility for the abuse (Goodman & Brown et al., 2003).

Due to the cross-sectional design of this study, it is not possible to infer directionality of the relationship between self-blame and disclosure. Thus, it cannot be confirmed whether disclosure reduces self-blame or vice versa. It is also important to consider that many participants in this study had not disclosed their abuse to anyone. Cisgender men are much more likely to avoid disclosing their abuse due to social stigma surrounding masculinity norms, rape myths that men cannot experience SV, and homophobic beliefs surrounding victimization by another male (Pratt, 2022; Smith, 2020). One study even found that male survivors believed that only the abuse of women was being verbalized and recognized and thus they did not feel safe enough to seek out support (Easton et al., 2014). Additionally, various cultural and demographic factors should be considered when examining the relationship between disclosure and self-blame. Sexual minority men are often even less willing to disclose their abuse due to gender biases surrounding SV, heteronormative views, homophobic attitudes, and societal acceptance of rape myths (Jackson et al., 2017; Rumney, 2009). Decreased disclosure rates are seen within the Black community due to years of systematic oppression, experiences of marginalization and rejection, and the general delegitimization of Black individuals as experiencing SV (Slatton & Richard, 2020)

Hypothesis 4b predicted that more unsupportive disclosure responses, as measured by the Checklist of Sexual Abuse and Related Stressors (CSARS), would predict self-blame, as measured by the Rape Attribution Questionnaire (RAQ). This prediction was also not supported, but similar to the other hypotheses, there was a strong positive correlation between unsupportive disclosure responses and self-blame. The most likely reason for this finding is that this hypothesis had insufficient power to detect a true prediction. Due to many participants having never disclosed their CSA and/or ASA events, this study was only able to obtain 64 individuals who had previously disclosed; initial a priori analyses predicted a sample size of 70 to obtain a medium effect size.

The current study's findings are contradictory to previous research which have found supportive disclosure experiences to often be related to lower levels of self-blame (Dworkin et al., 2019). Positive disclosure experiences have also been tied to increased self-worth, self-esteem, and feeling of acceptance, which likely relate to less experiences of trauma-related self-blame (Littleton, 2010). On the other end, unsupportive or negative disclosure responses involving blaming, attempts at control, distraction, and treating survivors differently lead to significantly worse psychopathology (Dworkin et al., 2019). Additionally, some studies have found that negative responses from others had a much larger impact on symptoms and well-being than positive responses, and Black individuals were more likely to experience negative responses than their White peers (Jacques-Tiura et al., 2010). According to research, for female survivors, supportive disclosure responses occur approximately 60% of the time, but rates for male survivors are unknown (Grandgenett et al., 2020). Due to gender biases and stigmatization still surrounding male survivors of SV, it can be assumed these rates may be lower for men, thus further preventing them from disclosing.

In this study, out of 179 participants included in the sample, only 36% reported having previously disclosed their nonconsensual sexual event. This disclosure rate is slightly higher than previous studies which have found that approximately 26% of men disclose (Easton, 2012). One possible reason for this slightly higher disclosure rate, was the presence of primarily White men in the sample. Previous research has found that White individuals are more likely to disclose than individuals of color (Slatton & Richard, 2020). Other important factors to consider as potential barriers to disclosure are high religiosity, gender and sexual minority status, and ethnic and racial minority status (Easton et al., 2014; Shaw et al., 2001; Zalcberg, 2017). Additionally, individuals in this study were a subset of male survivors of SV; those who were willing to identify as survivors, thus there may be a level of selection bias. The findings from this research only further reinforce the importance of continued trauma-related research, especially with individuals holding multiple minority identities and male gender. Additionally, this research supports the need for continued research that provides survivors a way to anonymously disclose with the opportunity to receive important psychoeducation like what was provided in the debriefing forms of this study. Research has found that anonymous disclosures, which have been spurred by the #MeToo movement, can lead to feelings of increased emotional support, connectedness, and act as an antidote to self-blame and shame (Gueta et al., 2020)

Hypothesis 5 predicted that survivors who consumed any drugs or alcohol prior to the CSA or ASA incident would endorse significantly higher levels of self-blame, as measured by the Rape Attribution Questionnaire (RAQ), than those who did not consume any substances. This prediction was supported in the present study. Much of the previous research on substance use and SV supports these findings. Research has shown that survivors who were under the influence at the time of the assault and then reported their abuse, were often revictimized by the dismissive responses, lack of support, and victim blaming behaviors, which all led to increased self-blame and guilt (Mennicke et al., 2019). Further confirmation of these findings is supported by research that shows male survivors who are intoxicated at the time of their nonconsensual sexual event are even less likely to disclose their abuse, which often leads to them getting stuck in the cycle of revictimization and self-blame (Sivagurunathan et al., 2019). Lastly, one study found that individuals who ingested drugs reported severe violence during their assault and had worse mental health outcomes (O'Callaghan & Ullman, 2021).

Although there have been findings to support the results of this study, some of the past research also contradicts these findings. There has still been some split regarding the impact of substance use on the development of PTSD symptoms, self-blame, and overall psychological outcomes. Some research has found that substance intoxication may act as a protective factor due to the memory encoding processes that may be disrupted because of the substance (O'Callaghan & Ullman, 2021) and result in fewer PTSD symptoms (Gong et al., 2019). The findings from this study aid in further supporting substance intoxication as having negative effects on psychological well-being and self-blame. Additionally, this study expanded on previous research by using an online survey method, focusing on male survivors, and targeting a slightly more diverse group of participants.

This study did not make distinctions regarding what type(s) of substances were used, whether the substances were consumed voluntarily or without the participants' knowledge/consent, how intoxicated the survivor was, and how close to the event the substance was ingested. Previous research has revealed that these specific distinctions may be incredibly important for understanding the differences in outcomes for survivors. Certain substances or level of intoxication may dampen the stress-response, meaning there is a potential for survivors to experience less symptom severity (Levenson et al., 1980). One of the most important factors to consider when discussing substance intoxication during a nonconsensual sexual event is whether it may impact the survivor's willingness to disclose or the likelihood of any legal actions being taken against the perpetrator, and how both of these factors may impact the well-being of the survivor (Relyea & Ullman, 2015). Survivors may be hesitant to disclose if they chose to be under the influence, due to societal beliefs that these survivors purposefully put themselves in an altered state of mind, which made them more vulnerable to assault and unable to provide accurate details about the event itself (Hammock & Richardson, 1997). Law enforcement agencies are also much less likely to submit survivors for rape kits if they were under the influence, due to their accounts being viewed as uncredible (Valentine et al., 2019).

Lastly, Hypothesis 6 predicted that stronger experiences of physiological sexual arousal, as measured by the Subjective Physiological Sexual Arousal Rating Scale, would predict self-blame, as measured by the Rape Attribution Questionnaire (RAQ). This prediction was not supported, but similar to the other predictions, a stronger experience of physiological sexual arousal was positively correlated with self-blame. Physiological sexual arousal is tied to activation in the sympathetic nervous system (SNS) and is part of the body's natural physical reaction, which is differentiated from psychological arousal (Bunderson, 2019; Hoon et al., 1977). Physiological sexual arousal has also been linked to experiences of intense fear/anxiety (Lorenz et al., 2012), which are common during experiences of CSA and/or ASA (Gilmore et al., 2010).

The findings from this study do not necessarily closely align with previous research. Past studies have found that physiological sexual arousal, orgasm, and ejaculation are common experiences for both male and female survivors of SV (Gilmore et al., 2010; Levin & van Berlo, 2004). Research has also shown that individuals who experience sexual arousal and/or orgasm are much less likely to report their assault to law enforcement agencies due to fears surrounding the possibility of these details being brought up during an investigation, which often lead to higher rates of self-blame (Bullock & Beckson, 2011; Bunderson, 2019). Due to so few individuals understanding the differences between physiological and psychological sexual arousal, and the uncontrollable nature of physiological arousal, survivors are often confused about the nature of the event, which can increase rates of unacknowledged rape, and decrease the likelihood of legal consequences for the perpetrator (Yun & Michael, 2021).

The incongruence seen between the findings of this research and past studies may be attributed to various factors. One potential reason for these findings is that participants may not have a clear memory of the specific physiological responses during their event, due to how long it has been since they experienced the abuse/assault. Another potential reason is participants may have been confused by the descriptions or wording of certain questions on the Subjective Physiological Sexual Arousal Scale. Although this scale has been used in previous research, many researchers argue there is no effective way to measure physiological arousal through self-report methods due to lack of self-awareness, embarrassment, or other factors (Mosher et al., 2010). The argument can also be made that these findings are just a true representation of the experiences of this specific sample; for them, physiological sexual arousal is not predictive of trauma-related self-blame.

Clinical and Theoretical Implications

This study aimed to increase the available research regarding factors contributing to self-blame in male survivors of sexual victimization. The hope is this research will provide valuable information regarding the unique experiences of men who survive SV to help inform therapeutic interventions, policy change, and further research.

The findings of this research highlight how imperative it is to address, normalize, and provide psychoeducation about the variables discussed in this study, especially the less well-known phenomenon such as physiological sexual arousal and TI. Due to the high endorsement of self-blame within this study, it is apparent many survivors of CSA and ASA likely have similar experiences. It is important to consider how stigmatized many of these topics are, which decreases the likelihood individuals will bring these experiences up in therapy spontaneously. Thus, it is imperative that treatment providers educate themselves on these topics and become comfortable addressing them with clients, to increase the likelihood that self-blame cognitions can be targeted throughout treatment.

The current trauma-focused therapies in regular circulation do not directly address any of these self-blame predictors, nor are there specific approaches to address TI and physiological sexual arousal experienced during rape. More recent research is starting to explore the use of somatic-based therapies to address assault trauma involving TI, which includes specific exercises and movements, body awareness training, and breathing techniques (Stirling & Andrews, 2021). Other research is focusing on a psychoeducational-based interventions to address TI experiences with veteran and active-duty populations (Morabito, 2022). Additional research has displayed the importance of multi-disciplinary treatment for survivors who experienced TI, which includes physiotherapists who focus solely on body-based interventions (Raj & Chowdhury, 2022). All these new studies have only been conducted using qualitative methods with a few participants and thus more research is needed to determine the effectiveness of these interventions.

Another apparent issue within treating survivors of SV is the fear and anxiety surrounding disclosure. Research has shown that survivors are often still concerned about disclosing their trauma even with therapists or other healthcare professionals (Jacques-Tiura et al., 2010). Since there is still so much shame and blame infused into survivors' experiences, therapists and other clinicians need to take the first step in addressing these topics. Therapists must provide psychoeducation and normalize the involuntary nature of TI and physiological arousal while also discussing and dismissing rape myths. This may then open the door for survivors to share more specific details about their own experiences. Some research has shown survivors are more willing to engage in anonymous disclosure through platforms such as Tumblr,

Twitter, and Reddit which may result in some level of peer social support (Andalibi et al., 2016; Mendes et al., 2019).

There is also a newer psychotherapy approach that seeks to directly address guilt and shame for survivors of traumatic events, known as Trauma-Informed Guilt Reduction (TrIGR). This therapeutic approach focuses on directly exploring and targeting guilt and self-blame by helping clients to recognize the reality of what they actually knew leading up to their traumatic event, and what they were truly capable of doing during their experience (Capone et al., 2021). Other research is exploring how mindfulness-based therapies can address self-blame through the use of self-acceptance and self-compassion (Szoke & Hazlett-Stevens, 2019). Although there is utility in this approach, clinicians should assure they are thoroughly addressing the self-blame cognitions and providing extensive psychoeducation alongside the other interventions.

Therapists also need to be aware that even when other trauma-related symptoms abate, self-blame may still remain even after treatment has concluded. Some research has found that even after completion of trauma-specific therapy, Cognitive Processing Therapy (CPT), a large portion of the sample were still experiencing significant levels of self-blame (Larsen et al., 2018). Within this treatment modality, there is room to address self-blame cognitions, especially if they arise as "stuck points" for clients, but the manualized instructions of this approach do not directly guide clinicians to explore self-blame. Thus, only those clinicians who are aware of the prevalence of self-blame and readily recognize self-blame cognitions from their clients are likely to address it.

Another important factor to consider when discussing the implications of this research is the necessity for wider spread psychoeducation on common experiences during CSA and ASA. As so much of the past and current research shows, including this study, survivors are often unwilling or unable to disclose their abuse and thus do not receive the services they need. Much of the hesitancy to disclose is tied to the stigma surrounding experiences and beliefs such as TI, physiological sexual arousal, and rape myth acceptance. In order to start destigmatizing these experiences, psychoeducation needs to be provided to the more general public. The findings of this study, reinforce the importance of providing psychoeducation on rape myths, substance use, and disclosure, as these factors were all seen to lead to higher rates of self-blame. This education could start as early as elementary school, since the rates of CSA are staggering. It can involve discussions with teachers, parents, caregivers, family members, and other individuals directly involved in children's' lives; helping them understand the importance of this knowledge. Seminars and trainings should also be happening at the administrative and higher education levels to assure this information is being dispersed as widely as possible. The more these experiences are de-mystified and de-stigmatized, the more likely it is that survivors will reach out for support and be able to address the self-blame and psychological distress that has arisen because of their abuse.

Additional changes and education need to happen at the state and federal levels for those who are responsible for policy changes and laws. There is still so much variety in the legal definitions of consent, rape, and sexual abuse. Without a consistent definition, survivors may not immediately recognize what happened to them as a nonconsensual sexual event, which may lead to unacknowledged rape, which then increases rates of rape myth acceptance and eventually self-blame. Many states still hold strict reporting laws regarding the timeline to report assault and/or abuse, otherwise the perpetrator may be given a much lower charge. Biases and prejudice also still exist within law enforcement agencies which often leads to increased delegitimization of male rape (Angelone et al., 2020). Additionally, the high levels of rape myth acceptance, especially regarding the myth "men cannot be raped" also lead law enforcement agencies to believe men are more likely to make false reports of rape than women (Walfield, 2020). It is also important to consider the high rates of TI, physiological sexual arousal, and substance use that were found in this study. Many survivors believe that any/all of these factors lead to less credibility if they were to report their assault (Bovin et al., 2014; Bullock & Beckson, 2011; Lorenz & Ullman, 2016). The unfortunate truth is the rates of legal follow through with rape cases is incredibly low; with only 12% leading to arrest, 9% being prosecuted, and only 5% resulting in felony conviction (Hine & Murphy, 2019). Even more unfortunate, is the fact these statistics are likely only representative of female rape victims and do not encompass the experiences of male survivors. It can be hypothesized the rates for males are likely even lower.

Research Strengths and Limitations

Strengths

The current study added to the limited research on predictive factors of self-blame in male survivors of sexual trauma and addressed many factors that have yet to be formally explored in research. This appears to be the first study to include this combination of factors in both CSA and ASA male survivors exclusively, as so much of the previous research has focused on female survivors only or a combination of male and female survivors. Additionally, this study was able to provide evidence that acceptance of rape myths is a strong predictor of self-blame for male survivors even when so many of the common rape myths circulating in society are gender biased, labeling men as the perpetrators rather than the victims. This is important information considering how many people still strongly believe the rape myth that men cannot be raped. Lastly, important information was gathered regarding the strong correlation between physiological sexual arousal and self-blame. This is not a topic that has been thoroughly investigated in previous research due to the stigmatization surrounding asking these types of questions related to SV/unwanted sexual experiences. This finding is especially important for individuals with male genitalia as rates of unwanted arousal and ejaculation tend to be much higher than for individuals with female genitalia.

A major strength of this study is that it utilized psychometrically strong questionnaires that also demonstrated high internal consistency in the current project. Every measure used in this study has been used in previous research and found to be a valid measure of the factor it is addressing. This is especially important for future research related to this topic as it can be easily replicated using these measures which are all self-report and not copyrighted. Additionally, a fairly large sample was recruited, although the number was slightly below what was initially hoped for to establish sufficient power. A post hoc power analysis revealed there was still sufficient power to run all the required analyses. The statistical findings also revealed large effect sizes indicating the findings from this research are more likely to have important clinical relevance.

Another strength of this study was that it was thoughtfully designed in a manner that provided basic psychoeducation to anyone who attempted to take or completed the survey regarding many common experiences. For example, the debrief forms provided information normalizing physiological sexual arousal and TI and provided information on how these experiences are completely out of the control of the individual, which could potentially reduce some of the self-blame these survivors are experiencing. Additionally, the end of the survey provided further psychoeducation on self-blame and how although it is a normal and understandable response for survivors, it is not indicative of them holding any blame or responsibility for what was done to them, and rather appropriately shifts the blame to the perpetrator.

Another strength of this study is that it directly expanded upon previous research using many identical measures, with similar research questions, and a similar population. This is a strength due to the fact that it helped further solidify the findings from the previous study (Pratt, 2022) while also expanding the findings to a new gender identity group which increases the generalizability of these the results overall. By identifying both the strengths and weaknesses of the previous study, this research was able to be improved through the process of trial and error.

A final strength of this study was the use of an online survey design which allowed for a larger group of participants to be accessed compared to when using a more traditional paper survey method. Due to this study design, a more diverse demographic group and nationwide sample was able to be obtained much more quickly than with more traditional methods. Additionally, the survey was designed through the Qualtrics platform which is known for its user-friendly nature and cellular optimization. Using this platform increased the likelihood that individuals who did not have access to a laptop would still be able to complete the survey using their cellular device, which further expanded the accessibility of the study and likely contributed to a slightly more diverse sample.

Limitations

This study has several limitations. Although multiple validity checks were utilized to improve the quality of data gathered through an online platform, there are still potential pitfalls with this data collection method. There was no definitive way to assure participants were answering honestly and providing true information on their actual experiences. Additionally, data gathering through an online platform limits individuals who can be part of the study to those who have internet access and have previously registered as workers through the MTurk platform, which may exclude some individuals who would otherwise meet the criteria for this study.

Another noted limitation of this study was the use of exclusively self-report measures. Although this is common practice in psychological research there are still some concerns with this method of data collection. With self-report measures, participants may respond in a more positive manner in order to present a certain image of themselves, known as positive impression management, or they may not have the insight and self-understanding to answer questions with total authenticity. Regarding measures used in this study, another noted limitation is the use of a self-report measure for physiological arousal. The measure used for this study has been used in previous studies but there have always been concerns on how self-report measures of arousal, especially after the fact, are not as reliable as physiological measures.

Related to participant responses, it may have been difficult for some participants to recall the exact details related to the nonconsensual sexual event experiences, due to them occurring in early childhood or years before in their adult life. This study did not directly ask participants to report the time since their last SV experience, and only required that it had been at least four months since their most recent. Due to a high number of participants reporting sexual abuse only in childhood, and the mean sample being approximately 30 years old, over a decade had likely passed since they had this experience. This could have made it especially difficult for participants to accurately respond to the sexual arousal and TI questionnaires, and remember other's responses to their disclosure, if it was disclosed in childhood. It is also possible participants had gaps in their memory related to the traumatic event, which is common in survivors of trauma.

Another limitation of this study was caused by the required IRB adjustments to the Sexual Experiences Survey – Short Form – Victimization (SES-SFV) which removed the option for participants to provide additional information on their experiences. Since participants were unable to provide information on the number of times they experienced each sexual event, what types of coercion were used during each event, and how many times they experienced SV within the last 12 months and across their lifetime, important data was not collected. It is especially important to explore some of these factors, as they could lead to important changes in clinical interventions and increased awareness for communities treating or supporting survivors of SV. Gathering data on the types of coercion used could have provided valuable information related to how survivors experience self-blame dependent on how they were manipulated by their abuser. The subject of sexual abuse/trauma still holds stigmatization even within the psychological, academic, and healthcare communities, as evidenced by the IRB's hesitancy to allow participants to be asked these questions. If these communities continue to consider questions surrounding sexual experiences taboo, survivors are likely to continue to feel stigmatized, rejected, and to blame for what happened to them, further decreasing their likelihood of seeking out treatment.

Regarding sample characteristics, although there was some diversity, especially in regard to sexual orientation, overall, the sample was very homogenous and did not contain a sample that was reflective of the U.S. population's true diversity. Much of the previous research has shown that sexual, racial, ethnic, and/or gender minority groups may be especially at risk for sexual victimization, and thus their unique experiences are important to understand. Additionally, members of these communities may experience unique types of stigmatization and rejection from larger healthcare systems and thus may be even less likely to disclose their experiences. Due to the demographic spread of this study, with the majority of the sample being White and heterosexual or bisexual, the findings may not be completely generalizable to many minority communities, which is a noted limitation.

Lastly, this study was a cross sectional design and thus has limitations regarding inferring causality. Although information could be gathered regarding correlation between variables, there was no way to determine cause and effect or directionality of relationships. A longitudinal study which evaluates participants at multiple points of times would be able to provide this type of information, however, that type of research design often requires an extensive amount of time, financial means, and participant follow-through, which was beyond the scope of this study. Additionally, due to this study only examining the experiences of adults who survived CSA, inferences could not be made about the unique experiences children may have after these events. Research with children requires extensive levels of protection, formal debriefing, and adds additional complexities due to necessitating informed consent be obtained from a parent or guardian, which could further complicate the child's experiences, and was beyond the scope of this study.

Conclusions and Future Directions

Overall, this study revealed that rape myth acceptance serves as a predictor for higher levels of self-blame in male survivors of CSA and ASA. Additionally, individuals who had not previously disclosed or consumed substances with in 72 hours of their nonconsensual sexual event, displayed higher levels of self-blame than those who previously disclosed or did not use substances. It added to the body of literature exploring self-blame in survivors of CSA and ASA by focusing on male survivors and examining multiple predictors which have not all been evaluated in one singular study. Self-blame has been shown to lead to worse mental health outcomes, including increased treatment resistance, worse PTSD symptomatology, and increased likelihood of revictimization (Bernstein et al., 2022; Breitenbecher, 2006; Ullman et al., 2014). This research provided evidential support that it is not just the traumatic event itself that may contribute to psychological distress and self-blame, but also events that occur before, during, and after the event.

Although certain demographics of this study were more diverse than previous studies, overall, the sample was relatively homogenous, thus the study was unable to capture the true breadth of individuals impacted by CSA and ASA. Sexual violence currently impacts individuals from all cultural backgrounds, with minority group members often disproportionally more impacted than their majority member peers. LGBTQ+ individuals are also at a higher risk of SV. In a sample of Black and multiracial individuals, 27% of transgender and gender queer participants and 14% of cisgender participants reported being forced to engage in unwanted sexual activities (NSVRC, 2019). Multiple individuals who identified as non-binary or other gender attempted to complete this survey, indicating these groups have a strong desire to share their stories as well. While research in this field is growing, so much less is known about the extent of the impact on gender expansive individuals, aside from the fact that they are much more frequently victimized. A qualitative analysis of LGBTQ+ college students found significant fears related to engaging with institutions (i.e., schools, police, etc.) after SV, and interpersonal concerns regarding disclosure, meaning these individuals were much less likely to disclose and receive services (Hackman et al., 2022). Additionally, Black, Hispanic, and Native American individuals are just a few of the communities that experience higher rates of sexual abuse and assault (NSVRC, 2019). Their nonconsensual sexual events are further compounded and complicated by systemic oppression and racism, rejection and stigmatization, and police brutality

(Slatton & Richard, 2020). Thus, future research should focus on exploring levels and predictors of self-blame across other ethnic, gender, and sexual identities.

The impact of revictimization or multiple nonconsensual sexual events across the lifetime is an important factor to consider when exploring self-blame, especially since so much of the research has shown a bidirectional relationship between revictimization and self-blame (Miller et al., 2007; Zink et al., 2009). In one metanalysis, an average of 47.9% of individuals reported at least one revictimization experience, with rates ranging from 10.0% to 90.3% across over 80 studies of SV in childhood (Walker et al., 2019). Additionally, the specific type of abuse, use of coercion by the perpetrator, and closeness of relationship to perpetrator may also lead to more severe mental and physical health symptoms (Pratt, 2022; Sanjeevi et al., 2018; Ullman et al., 2014; Zink et al., 2009). Unfortunately, due to IRB restrictions on this study, inquiries could not be made about the specific frequency, type, and/or severity of the abuse participants experienced, nor could they be asked about coercion techniques used during each experience of abuse. Future research should focus on exploring how these various factors may impact the self-blame experiences of survivors.

Additional factors to consider in future research include the identity and gender of the perpetrator. Previous research has found that closeness in relationship between survivor and perpetrator may lead to more significant symptomatology (Katz et al., 2020) but a study has not yet been done exploring how self-blame may differ based on closeness of relationship. These findings could provide important information for clinical intervention. It is also important to study how male survivors of SV experience self-blame differently based on the gender of the perpetrator. Since masculinity norms and sexist beliefs still exist, it can be hypothesized that men who are abused by women are more likely to internalize their experiences, leading to higher rates of self-blame and shame.

Although important research can be obtained from assessing the experiences of adults who have been through CSA, there is also unique information that could be gathered by directly assessing children and adolescents who are survivors of CSA. The complexities of using this protected population in research are not being minimized, but it is also important to consider how unique the self-blame experiences may be for this population when compared to adults. Some research has started to examine self-blame in a child population (Okur et al., 2018) but this research has not included other factors such as frequency of events, substance use, physiological arousal, and many of the other factors examined in the current study. Additionally, children may have unique experiences related to disclosure, including having to continue to live with their abuser, which may differently impact their trauma-related self-blame and other trauma-symptomatology (Jouriles et al., 2022). Future research should attempt to explore how the various factors examined in this study may related to the experiences of children and adolescents in the community who are actively experiencing CSA.

Self-blame is a common experience across various forms of trauma, although the rates are highest for survivors of various forms of SV (Spencer et al., 2017). Individuals who have survived combat trauma, physical violence, and various forms of childhood abuse and neglect may also develop self-blame cognitions (Jouriles et al., 2022; Lutz-Zois et al., 2015; Stayton et al., 2018). The self-blame experiences related to various forms of trauma and violence are likely to differ. Thus, future research could compare the difference in self-blame experiences for individuals who have experienced different types of trauma to inform therapeutic treatment.

Many effective therapeutic approaches exist for the treatment CSA and ASA. However, many of these approaches do not directly address self-blame and thus many individuals who complete therapy for SV still endorse self-blame cognitions upon termination (Capone et al., 2021). There have been some studies examining veteran's experiences of self-blame and the effectiveness of Cognitive Processing Therapy (CPT; Stayton et al., 2018) in addressing these cognitions, but none have been conducted on survivors of SV. Additionally, many clinicians do not have sufficient knowledge and understanding of the various factors occurring before, during, and after nonconsensual sexual events that may influence the development of self-blame, and thus do not know to screen clients for them. Future studies should examine the rates of self-blame for survivors of CSA and/or ASA both before and after trauma-specific interventions. Additionally, the field could benefit from research examining the knowledge base of clinicians working with trauma survivors to determine whether they are regularly assessing for and providing psychoeducation on the less well-known topics such as TI, rape myth acceptance, and physiological sexual arousal.

References

Abrams, M. P., Hons, B. A., Carleton, R. N., Taylor, S., & Asmundson, G. J. G. (2009). Human TI: Measurement and correlates. *Depression and Anxiety, 26*, 550-556. https://doi.org/10.1002/da.20462

Ahrens, C. E., Stansell, J., & Jennings, A. (2010). To tell or not to tell: The impact of disclosure on sexual assault survivors' recovery. Violence and Victims, 25(5), 631-648. Retrieved from http://0-search.proquest.com.library.alliant.edu/scholarly-journals/tell-not-impact-disclosure-on-sexual-assault/docview/817785178/se-2?accountid=25255

Amazon Mechanical Turk (MTurk; 2022-a). Amazon Mechanical Turk. *Overview.* https://www.mturk.com/

Amazon Mechanical Turk (MTurk; 2022-b). Amazon MTurk requester. *Amazon Mechanical Turk Pricing.* https://requester.mturk.com/pricing

Amazon Mechanical Turk (MTurk; 2022-c). Mechanical Turk concepts. *Requester UI Guide*. https://docs.aws.amazon.com/AWSMechTurk/latest/RequesterUI/mechanical-turk-concepts.html

Amazon Mechanical Turk (MTurk; 2022-d). Who completes the tasks on Amazon Mechanical Turk and how do they complete them? *Frequently Asked Questions (FAQ)s*. https://www.mturk.com/help#:~:text=Workers%20can%20complete%20tasks%20on,least%2018%2Dyears%2Dold

Amazon Mechanical Turk (MTurk; 2022-e). Worker requirements. *Understanding Requirements and Qualifications*. https://blog.mturk.com/tutorial-understanding-requirements-and-qualifications-99a26069fba2

Andalibi, N., Haimson, O. L., Choudhury, M. D., & Forte, A. (2016). Understanding social media disclosures of sexual abuse through the lenses of support seeking and anonymity. *Proceedings of the 2016 CHI Conference on Human Factors in Computing Systems*, 3906-3918. https://doi.org/10.1145/2858036.2858096

Anderson, A. B., Wright, J. D., & Rossi, P. H. (2013). *Handbook of Survey Research*. Elsevier Science.

Anderson, R. E., Cahill, S. P., & Delahanty, D. L. (2016). The psychometric properties of the sexual experiences survey—short form victimization (SES-SFV) and characteristics of sexual experiences in college men. *Psychology of Men & Masculinity, 19*(1), 25-34. https://doi.org/10.1037/men0000073

Anderson, L., File, T., Marshall, J., McElrath, K., & Scherer, Z. (2021, November 4). *New household pulse survey data reveals differences between LGBT and Non-LGBT respondents during COVID-19 pandemic*. United States Census Bureau. https://www.census.gov/library/stories/2021/11/census-bureau-survey-explores-sexual-orientation-and-gender-identity.html

Angelone, D. J., Cantor, N., Marcantonio, T., & Joppa, M. (2020). Does sexism mediate the gender and rape myth acceptance relationship? *Violence Against Women, 27*(6), 748-765. https://doi.org/10.1177/1077801220913632

American Psychological Association (APA), *Ethical Principles of Psychologists and Code of Conduct* (Washington, DC: American Psychological Association, 2017), https://www.apa.org/ethics/code/

Bernstein, E., Kanefsky, R., Cook, M., & Newins, A. R. (2022). Acceptance of rape myth and psychological symptoms: The indirect effect of self-blame. *Journal of American College Health, 70*(7), 145-162. https://doi.org/10.1080/07448481.2022.2086005

Beyer, M.S., Toumayan, A.C., Hipp, T.N. (2021). Sexual Violence among Sexual and Gender Minorities. In: Geffner, R., White, J.W., Hamberger, L.K., Rosenbaum, A., Vaughan-Eden, V., Vieth, V.I. (eds) *Handbook of Interpersonal Violence and Abuse Across the Lifespan.* Springer, Cham. https://doi.org/10.1007/978-3-319-62122-7_215-2

Bhuptani, P. H. & Messman, T. L. (2021). Role of blame and rape-related shame in distress among rape victims. *Psychological Trauma: Theory, Research, Practice, and Policy.* Advanced online publication. https://doi.org/10.1037/tra0001132

Bhuptani, P. H., & Messman-Moore, T. L. (2019). Blame and shame in sexual assault. *Handbook of Sexual Assault and Sexual Assault Prevention,* 309-322. https://doi.org/10.1007/978-3-030-23645-8_18

Black, M. C., Basile, K. C., & Breiding, M. J. (2011). *The National Intimate Partner and Sexual Violence Survey (NISVS): 2010 Summary Report.* National Center for Injury Prevention and Control, Centers for Disease Control and Prevention 2011.

Blayney, J. A. & Read, J. P. (2015). Sexual assault characteristics and perceptions of event-related distress. *Journal of Interpersonal Violence, 33*(7), 1147-1168. https://doi.org/10.1177/0886260515614560

Boas, T. C., Christenson, D. P., & Glick, D. M. (2018). Recruiting large online samples in the United States and India: Facebook, Mechanical Turk, and Qualtrics. *Political Science Research and Methods, 8*(2), 232-250. https://doi.org/10.1017/psrm.2018.28

Bovin, M. J., Dodson, T. S., Smith, B. N., Gregor, K., Marx, B. P., & Pineles, S. L. (2014). Does guilt mediate the association between TI and posttraumatic stress disorder symptoms in female trauma survivors? *Journal of Traumatic Stress, 27*, 721-724. https://doi.org/10.1002/jts.21963

Bradford, A. & Meston, C. M. (2006). The impact of anxiety on sexual arousal in women. *Behaviour Research and Therapy, 44*(8), 1067-1077. https://doi.org/10.1016/j.brat.2005.08.006

Breitenbecher, K. H. (2006). The relationship among self-blame, psychological distress, and sexual victimization. *Journal of Interpersonal Violence, 21*(5), 597-611. https://doi.org/10.1177/0886260406286842

Bullock, C. M. & Beckson, M. (2011). Male victims of sexual assault: Phenomenology, psychology, physiology. *The Journal of the American Academy of Psychiatry and the Law, 39*(2), 197-205.

Bronman-Fulks, J. J., Ruggiero, K. J., Hanson, R. F., Smith, D. W., Resnick, H. S., Kilpatrick, D. G., & Saunders, B. E., (2007). Sexual assault disclosure in relation to adolescent mental health: Results from the national survey of adolescents. *Journal of Clinical Child and Adolescent Psychology, 36*(2), 260-266.

Bullock, C. M. & Beckson, M. (2011). Male victims of sexual assault: Phenomenology, psychology, physiology. *The Journal of the American Academy of Psychiatry and the Law, 39*(2), 197-25.

Bunderson, K. (2019). *Female sexual arousal during rape: Implications on seeking treatment, blame, and emotional experiences.* [Unpublished doctoral]. California School of Professional Psychology at Alliant International University.

Buren, B. R. V., & Weierich, M. R. (2015). Peritraumatic TI and trauma-related symptoms in adult survivors of childhood sexual abuse: The role of posttrauma cognitions. *Journal of Child Sexual Abuse, 24*, 959-974. https://doi.ogr/10.1080/10538712.2015.1082003

Burns, B., Grindlay, K., Holt, K., Manski, R., & Grossman, D. (2013). Military sexual trauma among U.S. servicewomen during deployment: A qualitative study. *Contraception, 88*(3), 468-469. https://doi.ogr/10.1016/j.contraception.2013.05.144

Campbell, R., Dworkin, E., & Cabral, G. (2009). An ecological model of the impact of sexual assault on women's mental health. *Trauma, Violence, and Abuse, 10*, 225–246.

Canton-Cortez, D. & Canton, J. (2010). Coping with child sexual abuse among college students and post-traumatic stress disorder: The role of continuity of abuse and relationship with the perpetrator. *Child Abuse & Neglect, 34*, 496-506. https://doi.org/10.1016/j.chiabu.2009.11.004

Capone, C., Norman, S., Haller., Davis., Shea., T., Browne, K., Lang, A., Schnurr, P., Golshan, S., Afari, N., Pittman, J., Allard, C., & Westendorf, L. (2021). Trauma Informed Guilt Reduction (TrIGR) therapy for guilt, shame, and moral injury resulting from trauma: Rationale, design, and methodology of a two-site randomized controlled trial. *Contemporary Clinical Trials, 101*, 106251. https://doi.org/10.1016/j.cct.2020.106251

Casler K., Bickel L., Hackett E. (2013). Separate but equal? A comparison of participants and data gathered via Amazon's MTurk, social media, and face-to-face behavioral testing. *Computers in Human Behavior*, 29, 2156–2160. https://doi.org/10.1016/j.chb.2013.05.009

Centers for Disease Control and Prevention (CDC; 2020). Violence prevention: Preventing SV. Retrieved from https://www.cdc.gov/violenceprevention/sexualviolence/fastfact.html

Center for Disease Control and Prevention (CDC; 2018). National Intimate Partner and Sexual Violence Survey 2016/2017. *Summary Report*. https://www.nsvrc.org/statistics/statistics-depth

Cheung, J. H., Burns, D. K., Sinclair, R. R., & Sliter, M. (2017). Amazon Mechanical Turk in organizational psychology: An evaluation and practical recommendations. *Journal of Business and Psychology, 32*, 347-361. https://doi.org/10.1007/s10869-016-9458-5

Child Welfare Information Gateway (CWIG). (2021). *Child Maltreatment 2019: Summary of key findings.* U.S. Department of Health and Human Services, Administration for Children and Families, Children's Bureau. https://www.childwelfare.gov/ pubs/factsheets/canstats/

Chmielewski, M. & Kucker, S. C. (2019). An MTurk crisis? Shifts in the data quality and the impact on study results. *Social Psychological and Personality Sciences, 11*(4), 464-473. https://doi.org/10.1177/1948550619875149

Collin-Vezina, D., Daigneault, I., & Hebert, M. (2013). Lessons learned from child sexual abuse research: Prevalence, outcomes, and preventative strategies. *Child and Adolescent Psychiatry and Mental Health, 7(*22), 1-9. https://doi.org/10.1001.capmh7/1/22

Cook, J. M., Anderson, C., Simiola, V., & Ellis, A. E. (2018). *Journal of Aggression, Maltreatment & Trauma*, *27*(8), 867-882. https://doi.org/10.1080/10926771.2018.1446481

Covers, M. L. V., Huntjens, R. J. C., Hagenaars, M. A., Hehenkamp, L. M. J., & Bicanic, I. A. E. (2021). The TI scale in adolescent and young adult rape victims: Support for three-factor model. *Psychological Trauma: Theory, Research, Practice, and Policy*. Advanced online publication. https://doi.org/10.1037/tra0001000

Coxell, A. W., & King, M. B. (2010). Adult male rape and sexual assault: Prevalence, re-victimization and TI response. *Sexual and Relationship Therapy, 25*(4), 372-379. https://doi.org/10.1080/1468199100374730

www.ingramcontent.com/pod-product-compliance
Lightning Source LLC
La Vergne TN
LVHW090417210926
848480LV00002B/599